WRITE LIKE NOBODY'S WATCHING

Word Candy Productions, LLC

WRITE LIKE NOBODY'S WATCHING

M. J. SCHULTZ

First Printing: May 2024
First Edition

Spiral-bound book ISBN: 978-0-9861762-9-6
Paper Back ISBN: 979-8-9895825-0-1
eBook ISBN: 979-8-9895825-2-5
Hardcover ISBN: 979-8-9895825-1-8
LCCN: 2024909289

Interior and cover design by Ann Aubitz
Printed in the United States of America

Published by Word Candy Productions, LLC

ACKNOWLEDGEMENTS

For my fantastic grandchildren,

Cai, Coley, and Cade.

Believe in yourself the way I believe in you.

It's the best investment you'll ever make.

A special thanks to all my generous contributors:

Art/Design
Tom, Cai, Coley, Cade

Proofreader Posse
Susan, Crystal, Gloria, Cathy

Formatting/Printing/General Miracle Worker
Ann Aubitz
Kirk House Publishers/FuzionPress

TABLE OF CONTENTS

WELCOME TO MJ'S WRITERS CAFÉ!

✓ *LET ME ENTERTAIN YOU*

✓ *LET ME INFORM YOU*

✓ *LET ME INSPIRE YOU*

WRITE LIKE NOBODY'S WATCHING

YOU WANT TO GIVE WRITING A TRY. Wonderful! Perhaps you are reluctant to start because you worry about being judged. Maybe you doubt that your message is valuable.

My advice is to write like nobody's watching. Allow your muse (creative mind) to wander freely without worry or restraint.

The basic secret to good storytelling: Write from the heart, and your tale will evolve and ring true to the ear.

The world is in constant need of new stories. Why? Because we have an unquenchable thirst for knowledge. Storytelling is perhaps our most effective way of communication. It is the platform on which we share our valuable experiences.

We are wired to learn lessons wrapped up in entertainment. We seek out leaders and revelations through biographies, documentaries, and podcasts. We embrace novels and productions full of lovable and relatable fictional characters, then celebrate the crews who bring them to life with annual awards. We immerse ourselves in sports franchises, following drafts, investing in their dynasties, and reveling in their championships. We tune into *Dancing with the Stars* each week to watch celebrities evolve into competent dancers, voting for our favorites to rescue them from dramatic elimination.

We go to great lengths to share a group experience.

The classic themes for entertainment imitate the journey of real-life relationships and have remained the same throughout time. Forming teams and forging alliances within our communal circles is human nature. Lives are transformed through networking and collective struggle, realizing victory or defeat. Being a part of something bigger than ourselves.

Our desire to figure out who we are and how we fit in the bigger picture is at the root of it all. It is why we explore family relationships, question relatives, and dig into resources like ancestry.com to trace our origins. We long for purpose, to discover our best selves. This ambitious pursuit parallels memorable characters in the best fictional works.

Isolation is perhaps the biggest enemy of humanity.

Story-sharing gives us an immediate sense of belonging. It helps tear down the walls of separation, drawing the solitary into an alternate world of color, light, and hope.

Nothing makes me happier than to hear that one of my books helped someone through a rough patch of loneliness and extended them a bridge of community spirit.

JOIN ME IN MY WRITER'S CAFE!

I DESIGNED THIS WORKSHOP to share my trade tricks and encourage you to join the universal creative team.

You will never know if you can write unless you try. But once you complete a story, it exists for all time. It is a tale full of characters you shaped, living in a world *you* designed for them. What an admirable achievement!

While stories benefit everyone, the creative process is private to complete on your own terms. It is your choice whether or not your work ever sees the light of day (though I hope you decide to share).

I don't know where you are on the learning curve or which of my tips will support your project. If we happen to be together, I will ask you. If not, I encourage you to explore my café workshop on your own and take what you need, take what makes sense.

There is no foolproof way to write. There is no all-knowing teacher who has all the answers. It helps to study guides and test-drive their methods to see what appeals to you. It is also beneficial to read novels and view shows like an artistic insider, taking note of the strengths and weaknesses of their construction.

Meanwhile, dive in and begin! In time, with editing and revision, you will develop a unique voice and style.

A good writer never stops learning, seeking new strategies to make their projects more thoughtful and rewarding.

A good writer knows there is always room for improvement.

Storytelling is a magical experience. Launching into the creative zone to pour out your heart is joyful. The challenge is translating your vision into a format people appreciate and understand. You will learn a lot about yourself in the process. If your passion for the craft is genuine, you will forge on, no matter how tough the going gets.

ABOVE ALL,

WRITE LIKE NOBODY'S WATCHING

FICTION SHOULD IMITATE LIFE

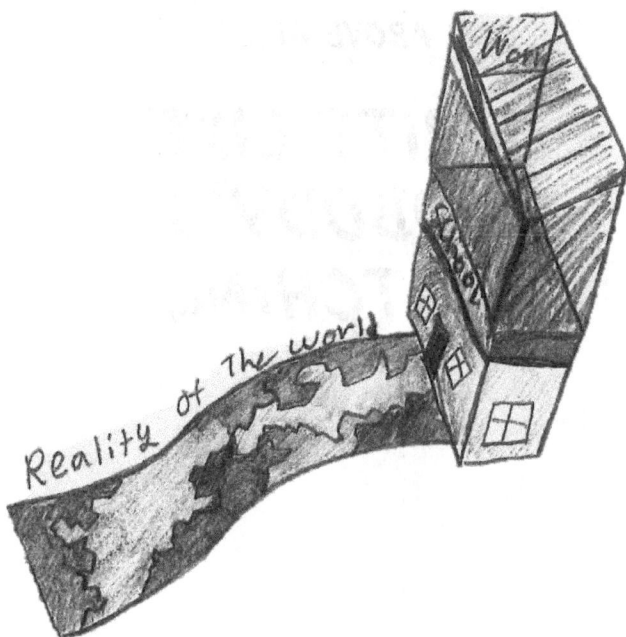

THE FANCIFUL ROAD WE'D LIKE TO TRAVEL

THE REALITY ROAD WE DO TRAVEL

GETTING STARTED

INCOMING SNEAK ATTACK

WE WILL EXPLORE STORY CONSTRUCTION from the ground up. I will demonstrate how Plot and Character interconnect on many levels to merge into one seamless structure.

While storytelling is an exciting process, beginning the journey isn't always easy. Take comfort in knowing that even seasoned writers often have difficulty launching a new venture.

Age-Old Wisdom

You can't make improvements to a blank page. But once you hit that page with some material, you've laid the necessary groundwork. Suddenly, it is a project you can develop.

Age-Old Starter-Scene Strategy

Sneak up on your misgivings. Study your concept and weigh possible story openers. Jot down any bits of narration or dialogue that could fit and see where it leads. I sometimes test-drive several opening acts before my plot thickens enough to dig into the body of the story.

RELATED TERMS

COMMONLY HEARD IN MJ'S WRITERS CAFE

- Protagonist/Hero/Main Character
- Antagonist/Villain/External Force
- Readers/Audience/Spectators
- Story/Production/Project
- Concept/Theme/Idea
- Special World/Fictional World/Fantasy World
- Real World/Actual World/Genuine World
- Central Characters (Large Roles)
- Minor Characters (Small Roles) /Walkons (Minuscule Roles)
- He/She/They
- External Conflict/External Force
- Internal Conflict/Internal Dialogue
- True Identity/Secret Identity
- False Identity/Imposter/Pretender/Mask
- Intermission/Bonding Break/Relaxation Pause
- Muse/Creative Mind/Inspiration/Wild Mind
- Endgame/New Reality

WHAT ARE WE DOING HERE?

We are crafting an attention-grabbing production complete with fascinating, relatable characters.

A STORY OPENS IN AN ORDINARY WORLD, offering a glimpse into the **Protagonist/Hero's** everyday life. Before long, however, new circumstances launch the **Hero** and other characters into a larger-than-life **Special World**.

This exciting **Special World** contrasts our **Real World** existence, where individuals often fall into boring routines while coping with studies, jobs, relationships, and health and financial issues. Unsurprisingly, an audience is eager to escape the commonplace through tales of adventure!

The goal is to coax spectators into a state called **Suspension of Disbelief**. They know the production unfolding is fake but choose to believe for the entertainment value. To accomplish this, a **Special World** should be unique yet still a place people can quickly identify with and imagine visiting.

Enhanced Characters populate a **Special World**. These characters should emulate genuine folks by possessing human qualities. Just the same, they are noteworthy. **Enhanced Characters** live supersized lives in the **Special World** orbit. A quest with points of conflict awaits them. They will face challenges that require initiative and courage. They aren't necessarily saving the world from mass destruction. But they also aren't merely doing their laundry.

It isn't necessarily the size of a character's goal that captivates; it is a character's enthusiasm for springing into action.

Enhanced Characters Speak Enhanced Dialogue. Characters should often talk more cleverly (purposeful and in shorter sentences) than real people because their statements must add value to the story and push the plot forward.

At the story's end, the **Hero** lands in a **New Reality**, shaped by the lessons learned on his journey.

A WORD ON SUSPENSION OF DISBELIEF

GIVE YOUR IDEA A FAIR CHANCE

ALL STORIES START WITH A GLIMMER OF INSPIRATION. And can lead to great heights of **delightful escapism.**

A **captivated audience** awaits, eager to buy into the incredible, unusual, and sometimes ridiculous to explore a new **Special World.** Put any doubts to rest by studying modern culture. Consider how often reality is truly stretched to the limit.

Imagine how a stranger to the planet might initially react to some of our popular entertainment. It surely would, at times, guarantee them asking: **"Seriously?!!?"**

Check out these famous concepts in the spirit of fun.

I am proud to be a believer.

Bluey (Animated Series, Books, Merch)

A worldwide phenomenon centered around a 6-year-old Blue Heeler dog and her fun, loving family. This series has an authentic feel due to its focus on social issues. Still, who could have possibly predicted this sweet cartoon's rise to the top of streaming platforms?

The Big Bang Theory (TV Comedy, Books, Merch)

A bunch of nerdy science guys exchange amazingly witty, humorous banter while somehow attracting—and eventually *marrying*, hot babes. They all mysteriously rally around the socially clueless Sheldon, who often makes their lives miserable.

Harry Potter (Books, Film, Merch)

Orphan Harry is invited to a magical boarding school to ride a broom, cast spells, and help hatch a dragon. Furthermore, he is already famous among witches and wizards because he survived an attack by the evil Lord Voldemort—*as an infant*! There are seven enjoyable books in this series, muggles. Who wouldn't want to own a cloak of invisibility?

Back To The Future (Film, Animated Series, Books, Merch)

Marty McFly travels back in time in a souped-up DeLorean at 88 mph to the scene of his parents' adolescence where his mom *asks him for a date*!

Diary Of A Wimpy Kid (Books, Film)

Undersized weakling Greg Heffley manages to survive the torture of middle school—again and again!

The Wizard Of Oz (Books, Film, Merch)

Dorothy follows a road made of yellow bricks in search of a way back home. She makes insecure friends and battles a wicked witch with a fleet of *flying monkeys* at her command! Only to end up missing her balloon launch departure. Luckily, Dorothy can still travel home via ruby slipper. FYI: this classic originated as a novel.

Star Trek (TV Drama, Animated Series, Film, Books, Merch)

The heroic crew of the Starship Enterprise travels faster than the speed of light to boldly go to wild places where no man has gone before, battling quirky aliens with agendas. The original 1960s show that spawned an empire is known for its deliciously cheesy special effects, costumes, iconic characters, and memorable taglines such as: "Beam me up, Scotty!" and "Kirk out."

I Dream Of Jeannie (TV Comedy)

A 2000-year-old genie *lives in a bottle* and turns astronaut Major Tony Nelson's life upside down with her good-hearted mystical shenanigans. Through it all, Tony patiently tolerates and protects her, often at the risk of his career and sanity.

Barbie (Toys, Film, Books, Animated Series, Merch)

Who would have predicted that a doll created in 1959 would endure as a pop culture darling for decades and spawn a 2023 *Oscar-recognized* movie featuring *humans*?

Murder She Wrote (TV Drama, Film, Books, Merch)

Mystery writer Jessica Fletcher somehow pumps out numerous bestselling novels while traveling the world solving crimes. Her powers of intuition and logic are nothing short of astounding as she sidesteps being killed by any of the murderers she exposes.

The Andy Griffith Show (TV Comedy, Film, Books, Merch)

The town of Mayberry is a magnet to millions of fans who see its low crime rate and colorful, lovable characters as an ideal image of an afterlife. Sheriff Andy valiantly keeps the peace no matter what goes down and inexplicably struggles to preserve the self-absorbed and bungling Deputy Barney's feelings and reputation.

Assignment

Consider the stories that offer you prime escapism. Why do you buy in? Spark fun conversations on the subject with your friends.

Read on as we discuss how to create fantastical, heartfelt tales full of conflict, passion, and derring-do!

STORY CONSTRUCTION OVERVIEW

There are various methods for constructing a story. However, there are specific components necessary to make it successful.

SEVEN ELEMENTS ESSENTIAL TO A STORY

1. Characters

2. Plot

3. Conflict

4. Setting

5. Point of View

6. Tone

7. Resolution

Characters

Characters are the citizens that populate a **Special World**. A **Main Character/Hero/Protagonist** stands centerstage in the production and has the most significant and urgent goal. An **Antagonist/Villain** is necessary to challenge this goal. A **Cast of Characters**, large or small, also supports the adventure.

Plot

Plot is a series of events that unfold in a story in segments called scenes. The **Protagonist** and other characters will take action to connect and reach their goals during these events.

Conflict

Conflict is the energy that sparks a good tale. Characters must struggle to hold an audience's interest. For the sake of drama, they must make some bad choices and come up against the bad decisions of others. The trick is to make sure they are *exciting* choices. The consequences of their choices push the story along and keep the audience asking: *And then what happened?*

Setting

Setting establishes where characters live and where story events occur. In-depth descriptions aren't mandatory (readers can fill in some blanks) but explaining where and when things are happening is necessary.

Point of View

Every adventure needs a narrator. The narrator transmits the story to the audience, offering a character's unique viewpoint/perception of everything that happens. A story can have a single narrator or multiple narrators.

Tone

A story is organically a comedy or a drama. It may occasionally blur the line and provide a serious situation with some funny moments or lighthearted fare with some downtimes. After all, that is how real life works. However, choosing a category early helps guide the audience to the proper mood. They are prepared to make an emotional investment but need guidance in the right direction: lightness in being or a depth of concern.

Resolution

The story wraps up here. This finale may or may not involve completely resolving mysteries and estrangements or reuniting separated characters. However, the audience must understand what has happened to everyone and why. The **Protagonist** must come full circle to land in their **New Reality**, wiser for the adventure. There should be evident growth in any central character.

We will explore how to best utilize these Essential Elements in the sections ahead.

THE JOY OF THE JOURNEY

AGATHA CHRISTIE IS A PROLIFIC AUTHOR who stands out as an expert on blending the **Seven Essential Elements** into entertaining drama. She initially set out to craft whodunits full of clever plot twists that her readers would likely enjoy once. What a low estimation of her impact! People frequently reread her books to this day, and knowing whodunit doesn't detract from their experience. Fans appreciate her stories for their notable sleuths, which are vivid and heroic, and for her skillfully structured plots full of intriguing suspects, clever puzzles, high adventure, and touches of wry humor. Filmmakers also repeatedly bring these story gems to life with a unique spin and various actors, retaining the characters and rock-solid story structures that audiences can't get enough of. She is a master we can learn from.

GOIN' FISHIN'

PAGE ONE, SCENE ONE

IT IS CURIOSITY THAT HOOKS THEM

IMAGINE CASTING A BAITED HOOK IN THE WATER and waiting for a passing fish interested enough to take a nibble. Now picture your audience in a store, library, or darkened theater, poised to consider your story.

The concept is the same: The first page of a novel, or a production's opening scene, needs an irresistible hook to reel in that potential audience.

Unfortunately, humans are a *fickle* bunch. Readers pick up a book, glance at page one, and often set it down with lightning speed. Theatergoers start to daydream if they feel disconnected from the opening act on stage or screen.

Luckily, humans are also an insatiably *curious* bunch. So, the trick is to engage their curiosity quickly. Spark the baseline question of *what* fascinating event is happening to *whom*?

ONCE HOOKED

IT IS AN EMOTIONAL CONNECTION
THAT HOLDS THEM

NUMBER ONE RULE OF STORYTELLING: MAKE THEM <u>CARE</u>.

THE YEARNING TO CONNECT with others is universal. We all want to *feel* something outside ourselves. The exchange of emotional energies fuels our hearts and souls.

Good fiction continually nurtures a relationship between **Special World** characters and the **Real World** audience. If your characters are interesting and relatable, the audience will plug into their emotional energies and fully invest in them.

Remember: The audience is eager and in place. Capitalize on their desire to participate, and you've nailed it!

HOW TO NAIL IT

GIVE THE BREATH OF LIFE

LIVE THE TRUTH OF THE MOMENT THROUGH YOUR CHARACTERS' EYES IN EVERY SCENE.

YOU ACHIEVE THIS BY FALLING IN LOVE with your creations as you write, encouraging them to act in their own best interest. The better you know your cast, the deeper you will love them. The audience recognizes the real thing when they see it. When you thoroughly enjoy their company, the reader will follow suit.

Assignment

Research a variety of opening scenes from novels and shows in various genres. Which ones grab your interest? Why are they effective? Do you like the characters? Why? Why not? Most importantly, do you feel an instant emotional connection to them?

GOIN' FISHIN'

ATTENTION GRABBERS

OPENING SCENES COME IN MANY FORMS. Sometimes, a tornado threatens, or a killer is on the loose. But high drama isn't necessary to spark curiosity. Check out the following examples.

- "You have *two* dates to the prom?"

- Nate reached into his pocket as he left the office and drew out a slip of paper. Turning it over, he discovered a message: *I know what you did.*

- "Stop! Thief!"

- "The police just called. There's been an accident."

- "This wine tastes bitter," Sherri moaned before collapsing on the sofa.

- "According to this letter from Dad's lawyer, you're included in his will."

- Sera opened the door to discover a bouquet of roses on the stoop.

- "I *dare* you to check out the cellar."

- The electricity snapped off, plunging Mark into darkness.

- The safe stood open and empty. Scott choked in terror. He'd been alone in the bank all night fixing the plumbing and hadn't heard a thing.

- "Your uncle *Fred* wants to sing at our wedding? Fugitive Fred?

- It was a dark and stormy night in Boston.

- "A naked man is streaking through our backyard!"

- "Take my car. Just don't look in the trunk."

- Megan searched her purse again. The lottery ticket was missing.

- Mama Bear discovered her cubs hiding in their brand-new treehouse.

- Caron drove through her old neighborhood with a warm feeling of nostalgia. Maybe she would try to enjoy the class reunion after all.

CONFLICT

FICTION IS FRICTION

VISUALIZE SITTING BEHIND THE WHEEL OF A CAR and trying to fire up the engine, only to hear the flat grind signaling a dead battery. Like the car, a story without **Conflict** isn't going anywhere anytime soon.

Imagine **Conflict** being the fully charged battery that drives your plot engine to high excitement levels.

THE THIRD C

So, you've managed to hook the audience. They are **Curious**, and they **Care**. The way to stimulate and hold their attention is by creating **Conflict**.

I bring this up early because it is so very important, for it is possible to unknowingly write a lengthy story without Conflict.

JUST ASK STELLA.

It was an honor to belong to an elite writer's group in the Twin Cities early in my career. Once a month, I was in the company of literary greatness. They were a generous group willing to share their talent and knowledge, which, in part, included critiques. We traded chapters to evaluate and sometimes read our pages aloud for group assessment.

Somehow, Stella's story-in-progress slipped through the cracks until after its completion.

Young Stella was a newbie like me. She had a talent for masterfully writing beautiful prose and nailing place and character descriptions—perfect qualities for the historical romance genre. The genre was hot then, so it was probable that Stella could make a sale. She got busy and wrote a 60,000-plus word sweeping love story. Stella fully expected to hit the big time, as many of us sold work to New York publishers back then. But Stella's downfall was that her lengthy romance hadn't a shred of *Conflict!* It was so sad to watch Stella deflate over rejection letters after months of hard work. She ultimately confessed that she didn't understand *Conflict*.

It was just that simple: she didn't know how *Conflict* worked. It had nothing to do with intelligence or education. She was a bright college graduate. To the best of my knowledge, she gave up writing, which to this day seems a shame.

SO, PRECISELY WHAT IS CONFLICT?

Conflict is a clash, a disagreement, a struggle, or a battle that will cause chaos in your characters' lives.

HOW DOES CONFLICT SERVE A STORY?

Conflict sparks the drama necessary to make a plot intriguing enough to hook the audience. It sends out a call for courage to the *Hero* and other characters. *Conflict* draws them out of their comfort zone to take a journey of challenge and discovery.

Think of *Conflict* as the deterrent preventing your characters from effortlessly getting what they want, the complications that disrupt the status quo.

A writer's job is to create a whole obstacle course full of stress points for their cast, only to resolve those issues by the story's end to the audience's satisfaction.

Meaningful, well-explained *Conflict* keeps a theater audience riveted or a reader turning pages, constantly begging the question: *And then what happened?* People struggle daily with life's problems, and it is human nature to be interested in the issues of others, to relate to those issues, and often learn from them.

Essential Takeaway

Emotion grows out of **Conflict**. Establishing and maintaining an emotional current between a character and the reader/audience is vital to ensure they care about the escalating **Conflict**. It is necessary to transfer a sense of passion and urgency to the audience throughout the story.

TYPES OF CONFLICT

Internal: The skirmishes between two voices inside a character's mind.

THE BATTLE BETWEEN HEAD AND HEART: the sensible choice or the passionate choice. A moral dilemma: right versus wrong, good versus evil. No matter the struggle, it all boils down to playing it safe with the known quantity or risking the unknown.

CENTRAL CAUSE OF INTERNAL CONFLICT: HUMANS' RESISTANCE TO CHANGE.

Humans instinctively hesitate to take risky action out of self-preservation. We all carry many burdens throughout our lifetime: guilt, loneliness, self-consciousness, dread of failure, brokenheartedness, and fear of commitment. You can assign any of these anxieties to a character to instill self-doubt and delay him from reaching his goal.

Bear in mind that you will need to personalize Internal struggles to make them believable to the audience. Drama works best when you convince the audience that the risk is realistic and stressful for a specific character.

Tailoring a struggle to fit a character's personality is vital. Consider that an everyday act for one person can be an act of heroism for another. A woman with agoraphobia might consider a walk down the street to visit a sick friend an impressive show of bravery. A clumsy fireman who agrees to enter a ballroom dance contest with his wife might need to muster five-alarm fire courage. An autistic teenager who joins an amateur theater group might feel the edginess of a first-time skydiver on opening night.

External: The obstacles a character faces that are generated by outside forces.

Life is a battlefield at times, caused by the pushback of others. Good fiction lays out one hassle after another caused by forces beyond a character's control.

A mean-spirited boss, a neglectful doctor, a stubborn relative, a disloyal friend, an extreme survivalist, or a cop focused on making an arrest can all generate turmoil. It can be a hassle caused by an institution or an organization. Or it can be the trauma triggered by a car accident, a plane crash, an earthquake, or a thunderstorm.

Such **External** struggles, like **Internal** ones, should be tailor-made to fit your character's circumstances. It would be reasonable for a survivalist to be out in a severe thunderstorm, but hardly a case for compelling concern. But tossing the agoraphobic mentioned above into the raging storm would generate believable drama if she has a valid reason to be out, perhaps chasing her runaway dog. Placing the fireman at the scene of a minor fender-bender would be realistic but possibly too routine. But how about devising a car crash involving the autistic teen forced to suddenly drive her mother to the hospital? She has reasonable cause to be behind the wheel but will predictably struggle in the aftermath of a collision.

A Blend of Internal and External

Stories typically have both **Internal and External Conflicts**. For instance, a woman might be battling depression while struggling to keep her café out of bankruptcy. A district attorney might be facing a fear of commitment to his girlfriend while prosecuting a serial killer.

Essential Takeaway

Ensure any point of **Conflict** is compelling enough to attract the audience and is a plausible obstacle to which the audience can relate. **Conflict** should stem from an authentic circumstance and not just be planted to make an over-the-top splash.

CONFLICT DEVELOPMENT

TWO STORIES

THREE ESCALATING LEVELS OF CONFLICT

TRACK THE INCREASING URGENCY. But first, note how boring it is to have no **Conflict** at all!

SET ONE

ZERO CONFLICT

A BEAUTIFUL DAY IN THE NEIGHBORHOOD

Twelve-year-old Amanda awoke at 7:30 a.m., shut off her alarm, washed up, styled her hair, and carefully chose an outfit for school. She then skipped to the kitchen where her mom, singing a cool Taylor Swift tune, set out orange juice and cereal doused with milk for her and her baby sister Beth. Amanda ate, collected her backpack, patted Beth's head, caught the kiss Mom blew her way, and then strolled to the school bus stop. The bus rolled up to the corner on time at 8:10 a.m. The folding doors opened to reveal her cheery driver, Matt. Amanda climbed aboard and greeted Matt and several other jolly classmates. Her best friend Ella had reserved their usual seat in the rear. Amanda plopped beside her with a grin and accepted the giant chocolate chip cookie Ella brought her regularly.

MODERATE CONFLICT

A SO-SO DAY IN THE NEIGHBORHOOD

Twelve-year-old Amanda slept through her alarm until 7:50 a.m., putting her twenty minutes behind schedule. She dove out of bed only to stub her toe on a chair leg. Ouch! She then hobbled to the bathroom to wash up, brush her hair, and haphazardly throw on yesterday's clothes. She rushed to the kitchen to discover her mom arguing with someone on the phone while setting out orange juice and cereal for Amanda and her baby sister Beth. Amanda gasped indignantly when Mom thoughtlessly dumped every drop of milk in the house over Beth's cornflakes! In an attempt to help, Beth slipped out of her chair and toddled over to pour Amanda's glass of juice over her dry cereal. Yuck. There'd be no breakfast today.

Amanda grabbed her backpack, flew out the door, and raced to the school bus stop, barely in time for her 8:10 pickup. The folding doors opened to reveal her driver, Matt, who was too busy reprimanding some unruly guys to acknowledge her with his customary grin. At least her best friend Ella had reserved their usual seat in the rear. Amanda plopped beside her, deflated to learn that Ella didn't bring a cookie to fill her empty stomach. And soon, the kids would start to notice she was wearing yesterday's outfit.

SUPERSIZE ME! CONFLICT

A ROTTEN DAY IN THE NEIGHBORHOOD

Twelve-year-old Amanda slept through her alarm until 8:00 a.m., putting her thirty minutes behind schedule. She couldn't afford to be late. Mr. Green was giving them a vital math test today—first period! Amanda dove out of bed and landed a bare foot on her baby sister Beth's Lego pile. The pain that cut into her tender heel made Amanda's eyes water. She hobbled to the bathroom, whimpering with every step, washed up, and then knocked her hairbrush into the toilet before she could use it. She fished out the brush, tossed it in the trash, then haphazardly threw on yesterday's clothes.

Amanda rushed to the kitchen to discover her mom arguing with someone on the phone while setting out orange juice and cereal for her and Beth. Amanda gasped indignantly when Mom thoughtlessly dumped every drop of milk in the house over Beth's cornflakes! In an attempt to help, baby sister slipped out of her chair to toddle over and pour Amanda's orange juice over her dry cereal, emptying half the beverage into Amanda's lap. *Double* yuck. There'd be no breakfast today, and now she had a stain on yesterday's pants.

Desperate to reach the bus stop for her 8:10 pickup, a wild-eyed Amanda dabbed her wet jeans with a towel and flew out the door. Still pampering her injured foot, she limped aboard the bus, idling at the corner. Oh, no! She'd forgotten her backpack! As the bus lurched into motion, she realized the driver wasn't friendly Matt but a sketchy man with missing teeth, foul breath, and icky body odor. Amanda stumbled up the aisle toward her usual seat.

Strangely, there was no sign of her best friend, Ella, anywhere. A glance at her watch established it was now 8:18 a.m. It appeared she'd boarded the wrong bus. And judging by the unfamiliar faces studying her warily, she likely was on her way to a mysterious location.

Scenario Three delivers the most significant sense of urgency and best begs the question: And then what happened?

- Are there bullies on the bus?

- Is the driver dangerous?

- Will Amanda ever make it to her school?

SET TWO

ZERO CONFLICT

BEST SUMMER EVER

Sam admired the Pacific shoreline through his trendy Foster Grants. He'd never felt a sea breeze so refreshing or seen so many cotton candy clouds in the bluest sky imaginable. He'd been King of the Beach atop his lifeguard stand at the exclusive Mayfair Resort for three incredible months. Now, it was Labor Day and the last hour of his reign. He'd return to college tomorrow with the fondest memories and an unexpected cash windfall. Due to a lifeguard shortage, hotel management had given him extra beach duty at double their negotiated wages, plus a suite of rooms. He'd been admired by the young male guests and pursued by the knockout girls who brought him daily treats from the chichi bakery across the freeway. Management gratefully acknowledged his unique charisma with the patrons. They insisted he socialize at the nightly bonfires and thoughtfully provided him with a nice suit to attend all the club dinners and dances. He couldn't wait to come back next year. In the meantime, there was a lot to look forward to. The visiting rock star's kids had promised to be in touch about hanging out over Christmas, and the local senator's daughter planned to visit him on Homecoming weekend.

MODERATE CONFLICT

OKAYEST SUMMER EVER

Sam scanned the Pacific shoreline through his budget shades. The heavy tinge of salty sea breeze and some gray clouds scudding across a pale blue sky suggested the chance of a storm. He'd been a constant figurehead on his lifeguard stand at the exclusive Mayfair Resort for three challenging months. Now it was Labor Day and his last hour on the hotel clock. He'd head back to college tomorrow with some tales to tell the guys and the wages he'd managed to save. Living costs had been much more than anticipated, forcing him to bunk with a fellow snoring lifeguard. However, due to a lifeguard shortage, the hotel management had given him all the hours he could handle and paid overtime. Also, on the plus side, employees were invited to buy healthy leftover meals from the kitchen at a discount.

He'd attempted to socialize with the affluent college-aged guests, especially at the evening bonfires, and had received, at best, mixed reviews. Some of them were friendly enough but not necessarily sincere. He suspected many secretly found his southern accent and middle-class status a novelty. There had been a fun, albeit brief, romance with the local senator's daughter, who, he eventually discovered, was merely using him to infuriate her folks. And he'd briefly clicked with the teenagers of a visiting rock star, only to inadvertently insult them when they drunkenly tried to swim in the ocean after hours. That confrontation had gotten a little dicey with security. He'd hoped to finish his last shift in solitude, but fat raindrops were beginning to pelt the beach. And shooing those rich kids off the waves with their surfboards was never easy.

SUPERSIZE ME! CONFLICT

WORST SUMMER EVER

Sam scanned the Pacific shoreline through his cheap sandblasted shades. The scorching sea breeze and the massive black clouds scudding across an eerily yellow sky screamed an incoming storm. He'd been a constant figurehead on his lifeguard stand at the exclusive Mayfair Resort for three cruel months. Now it was Labor Day and his last hour on the hotel clock. He'd head back to college tomorrow with a small duffel of tattered, sun-bleached clothes, a nasty windburn, and some pocket change. The cash crunch had been devastating. Living costs had been unexpectedly astronomical! For economy's sake, he'd slept in a dorm full of loud, smelly employees. Not that there was much time for sleep. Due to a lifeguard shortage, hotel management forced excessive hours on everybody—at straight pay. Which meant he couldn't begin to afford the discounted hotel restaurant chow and had to dash across the freeway to eat fast food every day.

Hotel management requiring him to help host their youth-oriented evening bonfires off-the-clock was another annoying shocker. Despite his best efforts, the experience turned sour like everything else. He'd hoped to befriend the affluent young guests, but most of the cool guys were generally snarky, and many of the girls mocked his southern accent and faded swim trunks. He had gotten involved with the local senator's daughter, only to discover a week later she was using him to infuriate her parents. When she was busted for curfew one night at a club down the beach, she blamed him, even though she'd dumped him days earlier. He'd briefly clicked with the teenagers of a rock star, only to have it implode over their intoxication and public nudity during his lifeguard watch. In revenge, they'd accused him of stealing some jewelry and electronics.

Security footage saved him in both unjust circumstances. Just the same, hotel management permanently branded him an all-around nuisance despite his hard work.

Unfortunately, the usual troublemakers still hung around the beach on this final day.

Soon, the black clouds swarmed in on dangerous gales to swallow up the sun. Earth-shaking thunder crackled, and bright lightning bolts cut across the yellowed sky. Then, down fell the fat, hot rain pellets. Alarmed beachgoers dashed for the resort. Except for some stupid girls—the senator's daughter included—who continued to paddle their surfboards out on the churning waters! Sam blew sharply on his whistle, only to hear the sound trail off in the wind. Management had blamed him for so much already. If anything happened to the girls... Sam frantically phoned for help, scampered down the stand's ladder, grabbed his equipment, and charged the turbulent surf.

He wouldn't set foot on this property again—ever!

Scenario Three again delivers the most significant sense of urgency and best begs the question: And then what happened?

- Will Sam end up in trouble with the management or the senator for the girls' stupid behavior?
- Will all the girls make it back to shore unharmed?
- Will Sam make it back to shore unharmed?

Essential Takeaway

Escalating **Conflict** pumps up the entertainment value of a story.

Determining how much you need to drive your story forward is simple:

Label your story's type and compare it to similar ones. It will help you determine the stress level necessary to captivate the audience. For instance, a children's picture book about a car race will cause less tension than a middle-grade coming-of-age tale. A romantic comedy will fuel a lot less anxiety than a dark suspense. A cozy mystery will generate less trauma than a horror story.

CHOOSE YOUR WRITING PROCESS

PLOTTER VERSUS PANTSER

WRITERS TYPICALLY USE ONE OF TWO METHODS to tackle their first draft. They carefully plot their story in advance, earning the title **Plotter**. Or they spontaneously fly into their story by the seat of their pants, earning the label **Pantser**.

PLOTTER/OUTLINER

A **Plotter** will outline everything they imagine will happen in their story. J.K. Rowling is an example of a **Plotter** who created her Harry Potter world in great detail. I confess to being a **Plotter** at heart. I enjoy the challenge of mapping out the big picture. I often create a storyboard with index cards or Post-it notes, a technique I discuss in the pages ahead.

PANTSER/DISCOVERER

A **Pantser** is an explorer who will leap into writing without a set plan. Stephen King has said to prefer this spontaneous style. A **Pantser** enjoys the thrill of charting an unknown course, discovering things about plot and character along the way. Imagine actors onstage doing improvisation. It's impossible to predict what they will say or do next.

PLOTTER/PANTSER COMBO

Being an inquisitive pioneer is beneficial when searching for your writing groove. Having a story mapped out doesn't guarantee a **Plotter** won't feel compelled to go offroad sometimes. And a **Pantser** must pause to plan when she writes herself into a corner. It's all about figuring out what works best in the moment. You may even feel the urge over time to outline one story carefully, then impulsively launch into the next one. Each project will take on a life of its own. Keep an open mind and go with the flow! There is always something new to learn about the process—and your talents.

PLOT VERSUS CHARACTER

WRITERS ROUTINELY DEBATE WHICH SHOULD COME FIRST in development, which drives the story: **Plot or Character**. Don't worry. This choice needn't be an issue. It's easiest to view them as equal partners in a project. They are co-dependent. A story needs characters, and those characters need something to do.

Essential Takeaway

No matter what you read or hear, there is no definitive way to tell a story. Sometimes, you will map out the scenes in detail; sometimes, you will fly on the seat of your pants so fast that steam will blow out of your ears. Sometimes, a character will inspire you, and sometimes, a glimmer of a storyline will ignite the process. Relax and let it all happen in its own good time.

CHOOSE YOUR STORY CONCEPT

(THE THEME OF YOUR PLOT)

"Where do ideas come from?"

"Where is the restroom?"

These two questions are forever linked in my mind because they were the most frequently asked at my book signings over the years.

For the record:

Ideas are everywhere.

And the bathroom is typically at the rear of the bookstore.

SERIOUSLY, AS YOU SEARCH FOR YOUR STORY IDEA/THEME, consider that fiction is written about folks by folks. Concepts stem from events that happen to people and how they react to those events.

In all things, get in the groove of asking *What if?* What if this happened? What if that happened? And then what happened? Eventually, inspiration will spark.

Pay closer attention to individuals in your proximity. Listen to the tales of friends and family (this is also helpful in honing dialogue skills), and mine them for ideas. Professional writers systematically do this. It becomes ingrained in your DNA.

Check out media sources. Newspapers, television, magazines, podcasts, radio, and the internet are full of happenings. You'll gather more concepts than you could ever write about!

Put a new twist on a book or movie. Or put a twist on a personal experience.

Keep a journal of ideas. Write them down *someplace*. I am notorious for scribbling thoughts on scraps of paper, but I know small notebooks are more practical, and I try to keep them handy. Perhaps you'll choose to put a memo on your phone. Or speak into a digital recorder. Just know you won't remember everything, so it is important to keep a record.

Don't ignore even the tiniest story spark. No concept is too small to consider. Tales often grow from a seed of inspiration. Perhaps it is the lyrics of a song, a scene in a movie, a sign on the road, or something someone said. I've written books based on book titles I fancied.

Tip: Expect ideas to pop into your mind as you drift off to sleep or even hit you in the middle of the night. Again, it pays to note these gems at the time. It guarantees a permanent record *and* allows you to unwind and return to dreamland. A flashlight at your bedside is helpful whether you transcribe your nocturnal musings with pen and paper or digitally.

CHOOSE A HERO/MAIN CHARACTER

- A STORY CAN HAVE MORE THAN ONE HERO
- HEROES VARY IN SIZE, GENDER, AGE AND TYPE
- ADORABLE ANIMALS & CARTOON CREATIONS INCLUDED

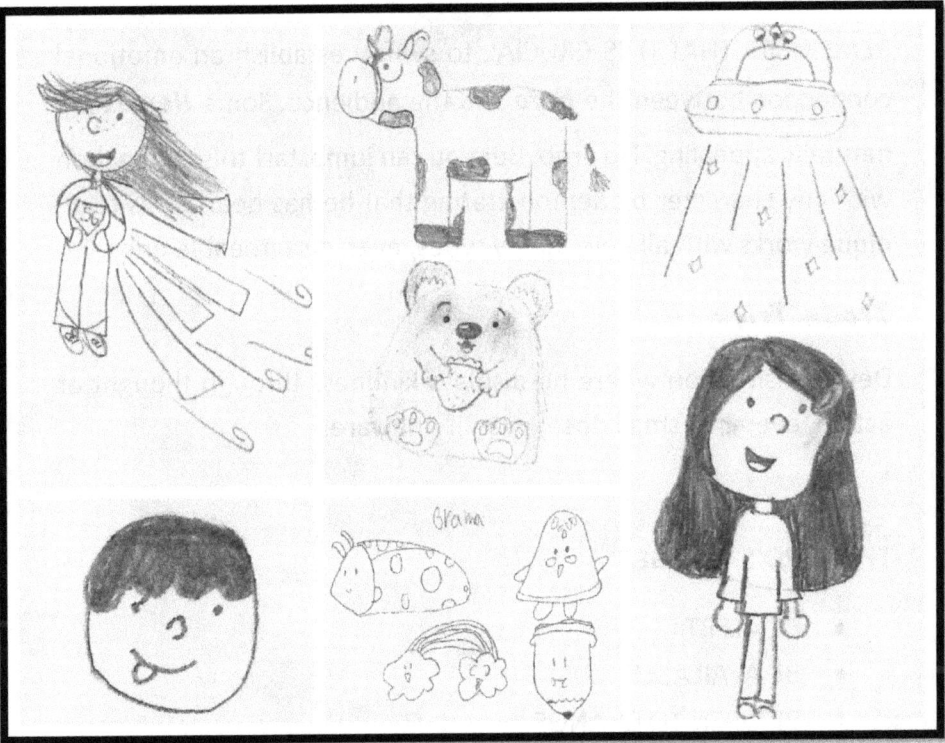

A HERO WITH HEART

REMEMBER THAT IT IS CRUCIAL to swiftly establish an emotional connection between the *Hero* and the audience. Some *Heroes* are naturally appealing. No prob. But you can jumpstart this connection with any character by demonstrating that he has heart. This technique works with all personality types, even disagreeable ones.

Trade Trick

Devise a situation where he displays kindness through thought or action, even in a small dose, even if unaware.

THE HERO'S PLEDGE

- BE ALERT
- BE AVAILABLE
- BE OPEN TO CHANGE
- BE WILLING TO SACRIFICE

THE HERO'S JOURNEY CHECKLIST

Be sure to pack him a moral compass to help guide the way. There will be challenging choices to make on the road.

1. A **Hero** must have a mission (desire) strong enough to drive the story and be fascinating enough to lure the audience in.

2. The audience should feel empathy for him *throughout the story*.

Empathy Strategies:

    a. Put him in peril. Not necessarily a dangerous situation. Any stressor that will cause worry will do.

    b. Create an opportunity for her to express regret.

    c. Invoke sympathy. Give him an undeserved lousy break.

    d. Make her pleasant.

    e. Make him wise and talented.

    f. Reveal his humility under fire.

    g. Assign her a weakness that makes her vulnerable.

    h. Devise a rescue or a gallant gesture, as small as comforting a baby, holding open a door, paying for a senior citizen's groceries, or leaving a large tip.

3. A **Hero** should be shown in conflict, bravely undertaking an obstacle course full of challenges as he fulfills his mission/chases his desire.

4. A **Hero** will ultimately have to make a risky choice to achieve her goal. The reader should share her stress, feel obliged to consider her options alongside her and worry about the outcome. The results need not be ideal. She might half-win and half-lose. All that matters is satisfying closure. Make sure the **Hero** and the audience have gained something from the experience.

Note: *Superheroes*—the *Batman* and *Wonder Woman* type—should be given magical qualities and assigned supersized challenges in keeping with their category's fantastical standards.

Essential Takeaway

Charisma is contagious in a great story.

A true **Hero's** lasting value is easy to measure. He fascinates long after all the plot twists are out in the open. The audience is anxious to return to his story and hang out with him in his **Special World**.

Members of your **Supporting Cast** can also benefit from possessing some heroic traits. Such charismatic qualities give them the same fascinating depth and likeability. Plus, well-rounded secondary characters are easier to write about than flat ones. You can devise exciting choices for them that create welcome plot twists.

Essential Takeaway

Giving any character a lingering heartbreak will make them especially memorable. It can be over the death of a loved one, a missed opportunity, or a careless act that caused someone harm. This device fits best in a drama.

Assignment

Consider books and productions that you have revisited multiple times. What specifically draws you back to a story? What qualities make the **Hero** and his **Supporting Cast** so appealing? Ask others the same questions and compare notes.

WHO ARE THESE PEOPLE?

CAST OF CHARACTERS

YOUR CAST DOESN'T NECESSARILY have to be complete as shown to be effective. Just make sure each Character is well-rounded and has a purpose. You may have more than one Character per category. For instance, you may have multiple Sidekicks or Antagonists.

CENTRAL CHARACTERS
PLAY THE BIGGEST ROLES

Protagonist/Hero – The character who is central to your story. The show is mainly about his quest to follow a mission and fulfill a want or desire. He will be taking the most significant journey of discovery and development. A positive person with a worthy goal and value system. Well-rounded with strengths and weaknesses, destined to evolve. Someone who will push the plot forward constructively, primed to battle a series of *Conflicts* thrown in his path.

Antagonist – A character with a negative agenda. One who works to prevent the **Hero**, and perhaps others, from reaching their goals. A troublemaker who supplies welcome **Conflict** to any plot.

Villain – A supersized version of an **Antagonist**. A deceitful or perhaps evil person. Someone who will stoop to dark methods to get his way and upset the **Hero's** journey. Some **Villains** are killers; others are tamer, depending on the genre. An untrustworthy person in all cases. Some stories have no true **Villain** but rely on **Antagonists** to fuel the **Conflict**.

Sidekick – A loyal person who stands by the **Hero** through the highs and lows of the journey. He is a relative, a best friend, or a co-worker. Like all people, he has flaws and can sometimes make poor choices. Ultimately, he is in the **Hero's** corner and knows him better than anyone else. He is a valuable go-between to pass useful information to the reader. Much can be revealed about the **Hero's** motivation through interaction with the **Sidekick**.

Agitator – A person who, for better or worse, stirs the pot at every opportunity to be noticed or even admired. Not necessarily a mean-spirited person, just an active one who will push the plot forward through her meddling. She sometimes reveals secrets, asks personal questions, or spreads gossip. She might be someone who likes the **Hero** and means no harm to him. Just the same, she is a skeptic by nature. She can, at times, openly disagree with the **Hero's** decisions. By doing so, she challenges the **Hero,** forcing him to question himself.

Mentor—A wise and moral person who guides the **Hero** on his journey of discovery. The **Mentor** might have a flaw or weakness that could eventually cause her to fail the **Hero.** Or the **Mentor** might remain consistently strong and upstanding in dealing with the **Hero.** Base the choice on which path best serves your plot.

SECONDARY CHARACTERS

Novels are peppered with **Secondary Characters** who play minor roles in your story. The **Real World** is full of people who provide us with daily interaction, and your fictional community in the **Special World** should also be. They rotate around the **Central Characters,** inhabiting their space and existing to add social variety and information. They are designated to enhance scenes with a bit of comedy or drama, sometimes moving the plot forward. They may be the familiar servers at the diner, the babysitter, the friend, the relative, the teacher, the parent, the cop, the bully, or the school principal.

These characters can be memorable in ways that readers love. You can make them odd, cranky, or heartwarmingly sweet. You can get away with giving them over-the-top eccentricities because they're not on stage as often as the **Central Characters** and a little dose of quirky can be more charming than tiring. Or they can be ordinary folk, well-placed to do a particular task or two.

SECONDARY CHARACTER CATEGORIES

Supporter– Helpful to the *Hero* in small interactions.

- The school guidance counselor encourages the *Hero* to apply for a scholarship.
- The computer geek offers to install a valuable program on the *Hero's* laptop.

Troublemaker – Irritates the *Hero* in minor skirmishes.

- The coach rides the *Hero* harder than his teammates.
- The self-indulgent relative borrows the *Hero's* car and doesn't return it when she needs it the most.

Impartial Participant – A mere acquaintance to the *Hero*, on the scene with little or no emotional stake.

- The flighty café server routinely gets the *Hero's* coffee order wrong.
- The neighbor often corners the *Hero* at the mailbox for a boring chat.

CAST EXTRAS

Walk-On—Blends into the background and likely doesn't know or care much about the Hero.

- The supermarket cashier runs the register.
- The minister officiates the wedding.
- The taxi driver supplies the ride.
- The deputy aids the sheriff.

CAST OF CHARACTERS
MASTER LIST WORKSHEET

Make a Master List of Character Names in this sample format to help keep track of them. Your Cast will be unique to your story, so some labels will differ. You may wish to add extra Characters to the list and eliminate others as you expand your plot.

Compare the names you choose to ensure none are too similar to confuse readers.

Expect to do some juggling! When you change one name, you may have to change others to keep them unique.

MAIN CHARACTER:

SIDEKICK:

ANTAGONIST:

MENTOR:

FRIEND:

2nd FRIEND:

BOSS:

COWORKER:

MOTHER:

FATHER:

SIBLING:

COUSIN:

NEIGHBOR:

CAST OF CHARACTERS
MASTER LIST *SAMPLE* WORKSHEET

Make a Master List of Character Names in this sample format to help keep track of them. Your Cast will be unique to your story, so some labels will differ. You may wish to add extra Characters to the list and eliminate others as you expand your plot.

Compare the names you choose to ensure none are too similar to confuse readers.

Expect to do some juggling! When you change one name, you may have to change others to keep them unique.

MAIN CHARACTER: Violet Hensen

SIDEKICK: Husband/Jared Hensen

ANTAGONIST: Neighbor/ Izzy Lewis

MENTOR: Mother's Sister/Aunt Sally Parker

FRIEND: Noah Andrews

2nd FRIEND: Harper Spence

BOSS: Kyle Grey

COWORKER: Desmond Frasier

MOTHER: Tess McCall

FATHER: Dr. James McCall

SIBLING: Ruby McCall Keller

COUSIN: Mindy Wentworth

NEIGHBOR: Robert Jacoby

CHARACTER PROFILE CHECKLIST

Fill out a worksheet for each Character. You can add details as you get to know them. It's okay if some worksheets remain incomplete.

Tip: Assigning a Central Character a Secret or Flaw will make them appear more vulnerable, relatable, and exciting.

NAME/AGE:

HERO OR RELATIONSHIP TO HERO:

HAIR COLOR/STYLE:

EYE COLOR:

PHYSICAL CHARACTERISTICS:

PERSONALITY TRAITS:

INTERESTS/HOBBIES:

OCCUPATION:

TALENTS:

WEAKNESSES:

FLAWS:

DESIRES AND GOALS:

FAVORITES:

SECRETS/FEARS:

LINGERING HEARTBREAK:

CHARACTER PROFILE *SAMPLE* CHECKLIST

Fill out a worksheet for each Character. You can add details as you get to know them. It's okay if some worksheets remain incomplete.

Tip: Assigning a Central Character a Secret or Flaw will make them appear more vulnerable, relatable, and exciting.

NAME/AGE: Ariel Green/27

HERO OR RELATIONSHIP TO HERO: Hero's Girlfriend

HAIR COLOR/STYLE: Red hair/Long

EYE COLOR: Blue

PHYSICAL CHARACTERISTICS: Tall/slender

PERSONALITY TRAITS: Fun but sometimes controlling

INTERESTS/HOBBIES: Golf, tennis, and reading

OCCUPATION: Law clerk

TALENTS: Great singing voice

WEAKNESSES: Chocolate ice cream and shopping for shoes

FLAWS: Hates losing at board games and is a terrible cook

DESIRES AND GOALS: To pay off her outstanding debt

FAVORITES: Old noir movies and 1000-piece puzzles

SECRETS/FEARS: Gave up a baby for adoption

LINGERING HEARTBREAK: Childhood sweetheart died in a car crash

CHARACTER CATCHALL
BEYOND THE WORKSHEETS

The worksheets are valuable aids to help define and organize your Cast. I advise you to take it a step further by assigning each Character space in a notebook to log any new personal information that arises as you write. Continuity is key in storytelling, and it is so much easier to refer to your notes versus paging through your manuscript to chase down a detail. You'll be so glad you did.

Take Note! Examples:

- New hairstyle or color. Describe.
- New car. Brand and color.
- Birthday. Current age and date.
- A couple breaks up. Who? Why?
- A couple starts dating. Who? Extra details?
- A move. Where?
- New job. What? Where?
- New secret. Specify. Who else knows?
- New flaw. Specify. Extra details?
- New talent. Specify. Extra details?
- New favorite food. Specify.
- Add a friend or relative. Name and relationship.

Essential Takeaway

Be on the lookout for how any new developments can support your plot.

Character Shuffle Using Index Cards

After I assemble my cast list, I assign each character an index card. As demonstrated below, I fill in the pertinent stats that I will refer to throughout the story. I use a pencil so I can edit them. I also color-code the names with various highlighters to more easily locate one in the heat of writing.

Name: Katy Smith
Age: 23 **Eyes:** Blue
Hair: Brown-Cut Short
Title: Hero **Drives:** Black Jeep
Job: Private Investigator
Home: Apt. on Elm Street
Boyfriend: Trent **Age:** 25
Family: Mom-Mae Sister-Sloan
Faves: Coffee & Chocolate
Secret: Won the Lottery
Best Friend: Amanda

KNOW YOUR OPPONENT

THE EXTERNAL FORCE

TROUBLEMAKERS PLUS A WHOLE LOT MORE

AS DISCUSSED IN **THE CAST OF CHARACTERS** SECTION, the challenger to any *Hero* is referred to as an *Antagonist/Villain*. But sometimes, more general terminology is necessary, and *External Force* fits the bill.

An External Force may or may not be a character.

The *Force* may be a situation, an institution, or a product of nature. Perhaps the *Protagonist* is lost in an unforgiving jungle, battling a shark or a storm at sea, pushing back against an unjust police investigation, or fighting a corrupt company.

In every production, the *External Force* directly opposes the *Hero*—and perhaps others—and should prove a worthy opponent throughout the journey.

About those Bad Guys in particular...

- Wise old saying: Villains don't think they're Villains.
- Antagonists/Villains justify their bad behavior like the Heroes do.

When specifically dealing with a **Character**—an **Antagonist/Villain**, note that he has what he perceives as a worthy goal and moral code despite his negative agenda, like the **Hero**. Often an equal match in terms of brains and strength, but destined to disintegrate as the **Hero** evolves. This disintegration occurs because he avoids painful self-examination, frequently blaming others for his misery and missteps. His narrow, negative outlook and flawed perspective provide rich sources of **Conflict** for any plot.

When first charting a Hero's obstacle course, it helps to define the External Force at hand:

- Subjective: Character-driven resistance
- Objective: Environmental or Institutional resistance

POINT OF VIEW (POV)

WHO IS TELLING THE STORY?
HOW ARE THEY TELLING IT?

EACH SCENE IN A NOVEL has a **Narrator/Storyteller**. He expresses what he thinks, sees, hears, and feels. In other words, he shares his **Point of View**/perspective of the situation at hand with the reader.

Many writers narrate their story solely through the **Hero/Protagonist's** POV. Sometimes, authors choose to include multiple narrators. In doing so, ensuring the **Protagonist** remains strongly represented is central. His well-being should be a constant priority to the reader.

THERE ARE TWO POV CATEGORIES

FIRST PERSON AND THIRD PERSON
I have focused on the four most common POV subcategories. There are some less common ones. Research them if you are curious.

THE BIG FOUR
- **First Person**
- **Third Person Limited**
- **Third Person Multiple**
- **Omniscient**

FIRST PERSON

One character, typically the **Hero/Protagonist**, tells the story. The plot is seen exclusively through his eyes. The reader gets his unique perspective on everything that happens.

This character refers to himself as **I.**

ADVANTAGE

First Person storytelling draws the reader in swiftly for a private conversation and full access to the **Protagonist's** thoughts. It is as if the **Protagonist** is saying: "We're good friends. I trust you with my innermost secrets and desires."

Sometimes, a charming **Hero** can make up for a less-than-excellent plot simply because the reader finds his voice appealing.

Many beginners find the **First Person** technique the easiest to tackle because it is like holding a real-life conversation, which feels natural.

DISADVANTAGE

It limits the reader to one character's experiences and opinions. They are unable to see anything that happens outside the narrator's scope. If the narrator isn't present for an event, it can take some creativity through action and dialogue to relay crucial information to the audience.

THIRD PERSON LIMITED

An **Outside Narrator,** not a character, tells the story. This viewpoint is limited to one character's perception, everything the character knows. This character is typically the **Protagonist.**

When presenting a story in **Third Person Limited,** each character is addressed as **he, she,** or **they.**

One way to describe the **Outside Narrator** is as a **Magical Genie** tagging along with the **Protagonist,** reporting everything the **Protagonist** thinks, sees, hears, and feels. **With a little something extra.**

The extra benefit to **Third Person** narration versus a **First Person** account is that the **Outside Narrator/Magical Genie** has the ability to pull the camera lens back a little in a scene to display the bigger picture. Perhaps, to note details of the landscape, like fluffy white clouds, the peeling red paint on a barn, or laundry flapping on a clothesline. Or to describe the **Protagonist** himself, such as his hair color, crazy socks, or limp. Any **Protagonist** *knows* about all these things but wouldn't typically think about them or report them on his own during **First Person** storytelling.

For example, a **First Person** narrator probably wouldn't step outside and say: "Gee, the sun shining on my brown hair must be giving it a golden hue."

But the *Genie* might report: "The bright sunlight gilded Jenny's brown hair."

ADVANTAGE

Third Person Limited, like *First Person*, places the reader inside the head of one character, but it also allows the narrator to pull the camera lens back for a larger view of the scene, giving the story more detail.

DISADVANTAGE

Third Person Limited often takes more effort to write than *First Person*. In *First Person,* you can get away with more *Telling* of events versus *Showing* them because of the fast-tracked friendship between the *Hero* and the reader. In *Third Person,* it is often necessary to *Show* more of the action to spark an emotional connection. (As explained in my *Show and Tell* section.)

This narrative is also more challenging to control. It is a common mistake to unintentionally hop into other characters' *Points of View.* These slipups then must be caught and corrected in rewrites because you are working from a single viewpoint; in other words, the thoughts of a single character.

THIRD PERSON MULTIPLE

An **Outside Narrator** tells the story through multiple characters, one at a time. The reader receives intel from various perspectives instead of getting the story exclusively through the **Protagonist.** Creating **Multiple Points of View** gives the reader a much grander picture of the story, taking in the knowledge and motivation of *all* the featured characters.

Each character is given a turn to take the stage and addressed as **he, she,** or **they.**

Limiting one character's viewpoint per scene in **Third Person Multiple** is wise. The reader may find it too jarring to head-hop back and forth.

ADVANTAGE

Giving a story more depth and drama is easier because you can shift **Points of View** to transport the audience to numerous scenes between numerous characters.

DISADVANTAGE

It is a more significant challenge to create several distinct voices in a story while ensuring your **Protagonist's** voice comes in strong and his goals remain clear throughout.

OMNISCIENT

Like other forms of **Third Person POV,** each character is addressed as **he, she,** or **they.**

This narrator, however, is set apart with his supersized God-like powers. He can head-hop like **Third Person Multiple** *and* float above a scene to add extra commentary assigned to no character. Such entertaining commentary especially sets the **Omniscient** apart. He sees all and knows all. He has information on everything and everyone and can reveal it at any point in time. He can even tease the reader with predictions because he is wise to the future! The **Omniscient,** while not a character, is a distinct personality with a voice.

ADVANTAGE

The supreme voice can easily feed vital information to the reader and make a story especially memorable with additional wit and charm.

DISADVANTAGE

As with **Third Person Multiple,** it is critical to create distinct voices and keep the **Protagonist** in focus. Plus, with so many added "powers" at your disposal, you are likelier to confuse the audience because the writing is considerably more complicated. Jumping all over the story map with numerous voices and options is a big chore. Also, skillfully pulling off clever **Omniscient** commentary is difficult and takes practice.

Notable Novels Written in the less common Omniscient POV:
- *The Land of Stories*, by Chris Colfer
- *And Then There Were None*, by Agatha Christie
- *The Westing Game*, by Ellen Raskin
- *Pride and Prejudice*, by Jane Austen
- *Harry Potter* series, by J.K. Rowling

POV-HOP: You will note in your reading that authors sometimes use both **First Person** and **Third Person Points** of View in a story. For instance, the **Protagonist** relates her version of events in the First Person, and the **Antagonist** relates his version in the **Third Person Limited.** There may even be **Multiple Third Person** narrators alongside a **First Person Protagonist**. This technique can be dramatic but is tricky, as it is necessary to bounce back and forth between the viewpoints without mixing them up.

Tip: Each POV-Hop is typically divided by a **Chapter Break** and sometimes a **Character Title** so the reader can easily follow along. Each character should remain in their designated POV throughout the tale. In other words, if the **Protagonist** relays events in the **First Person**, she shouldn't abruptly shift to the **Third Person.**

CHOOSE A TENSE

A STORY IS WRITTEN IN A **PRESENT OR PAST TENSE** format and frequently sticks with one **Tense** from beginning to end. It makes plotting easier, especially for novices.

MAKE SENSE OF TENSE

BASIC RULE: TENSE ESTABLISHES TIME

Verbs demonstrate *when* an action occurs in time, the **Present, Past, or Future.**

- *Present Tense:* Walk/Walks/Run/Runs/Pay/Pays/
  Attend/Attends/Watch/Watches/Think/Thinks
- *Past Tense:* Walked/Ran/Paid/
  Attended/Watched/Thought
- *Future Tense:* Will Walk/Will Run/Will Pay/Will
  Attend/Will Watch/Will Think

POV AND TENSE COMBOS

- **First Person/Present Tense**
  I quickly call for backup, then sprint after the suspect.

- **First Person/Past Tense**
  I quickly called for backup, then sprinted after the suspect.

- **First Person/Future Tense**
  I will quickly call for backup, then sprint after the suspect.

- **Third Person/Present Tense**
  Sergeant Dunlap calls for backup, then sprints after the suspect.

- **Third Person/Past Tense**
  Sergeant Dunlap called for backup, then sprinted after the suspect.

- **Third Person/Future Tense**
  Sergeant Dunlap will quickly call for backup, then sprint after the suspect.

- **Omniscient**
  Sergeant Dunlap called for backup and then sprinted after the suspect, not realizing a getaway driver was waiting for her on the next street.

You will notice creative uses of Tense in the novels you read. Some authors **Tense—Hop**, setting one scene in the past and another in the present, perhaps with different narrators. They sometimes get creative with a Prologue or Epilogue. If you decide to experiment, remember that a successful **Tense-Hop** dodges confusion.

Straightforward Example: A **First Person** narrator relates most of her story in the **Present Tense**, switching to the **Past Tense** to recount some events that have already happened.

Note: Expect to unconsciously and randomly **Tense** and **POV Hop** as you write your story's first drafts and synopsis. Your **Wild Mind/Muse** in high gear doesn't know the difference, just as it doesn't focus on correct grammar usage. It simply dumps intel onto the page as fast as you can transcribe it. Don't stop to make corrections. Just keep writing. Once you have the story arc loosely locked in, it's time to clean up issues.

GOOD DEEDS—BAD DEEDS

PET THE DOG
SAVE THE CAT
KISS THE BABY
OR
BURN THE FRIEND
BREAK THE LAW
STEAL THE GLORY

PEOPLE ARE GENERALLY GOOD OR BAD AT HEART. Just the same, they sometimes run an Internal Dialogue, considering options outside their everyday conduct. They teeter between satisfying their egotistical interests and tending to the needs of others. Their choices are often spontaneous and surprising.

As people surf daily on a sliding scale of good and bad behavior, so should **Characters.** Quirks, both light and dark, add authenticity and relatability to their personalities. It also makes them unpredictable. And unpredictability makes for exciting **Plot Twists.** What will he do next? Will she get caught? Will he get credit? *And then what happens?* The audience wants to know!

Switch things up with the lovable Protagonist and the irritating Antagonist. (All the characters in between qualify as well.)

Highlight a Protagonist's flaw—a minor one will do—to test her pure status as she pursues her goal. Create an Antagonist that is easy to resent, then toss in a redeemable quality—a minor one will do— as he works to thwart the Protagonist.

CHARACTER CURVEBALLS IN ACTION

SPONTANEOUS DECEIT

Reverend Ned Kemp spends Saturday afternoon sprucing up elderly Mrs. Wilson's yard. The congregation knows of her loneliness and her distant, ungrateful children. They care and try to help. When the clergyman finishes trimming the hedges around dinnertime, he enters the house to discover Mrs. Wilson has made them stew. She suggests they eat and watch an old movie on TV, as they did on Ned's last visit. Ned hesitates. He just got a text from a childhood pal reporting an impromptu poker game in the old neighborhood tonight. Ultimately, Ned can't resist the chance to shed his collar and relax with the guys who know him best. With a pang of guilt, he begs off over urgent Church business.

SPONTANEOUS REDEMPTION

Mick is a professional thief who makes a living passing stolen cars to a broker. Often the suckers deserve it, he rationalizes, carelessly overlooking keys in the ignition, sometimes even leaving the engine running. One day, Mick pinches a popular SUV worth twice his standard cut. As is his habit, he swings into an empty lot near the drop-off warehouse to loot the SUV's interior. The paperwork inside the glovebox reveals that a charity has leased the vehicle. In the rear, he finds two battered wheelchairs and a small prosthetic leg like his late brother's. Rare tears flow. The charity wasn't even careless. He broke in to hotwire the engine. For the first time, he reluctantly returns an auto to its owner.

MORE SPONTANEOUS DECEIT

- The typically reliable babysitter throws a party at the neighbor's house while her little charges sleep.
- The dedicated teacher drinks too much wine at a restaurant, carelessly leaves his students' exam papers in a booth, and pretends he accidentally destroyed them in a fire.
- The diligent traffic cop lets a speeder off without a ticket because she is married to a police lieutenant who can further his career.
- The respected advertising executive impetuously cheats an absentee co-worker out of credit on a project.
- The sweet third grader damages a book in the school library and then resists the urge to confess when the principal questions the class about it.

MORE SPONTANEOUS REDEMPTION

- The shoplifter risks apprehension when he stops to load a pregnant lady's groceries into her trunk.
- The phone scammer calls 911 when he realizes the dupe on the line is having a stroke.
- The crooked car mechanic offers the struggling mother of three a discount on a new engine.
- The judgmental neighbor resists the temptation to play favorites and buys cookies from all the Girl Scouts on her street.
- The school bully rescues a stray kitten from a busy intersection and takes it home to feed it.

Bottom Line:

Character Curveballs are optional. If you go for it, remember that often, all it takes is a little shift in conduct to round off a personality. Avoid extreme behavior swings unless you can establish a logical reason/clear motivation for it. The audience may grow confused or even feel betrayed if they can't generally classify a **Central Character**, especially the **Hero/Antagonist** duo, as good or bad through their actions. You'll risk tampering with the magical connections you've worked so hard to establish.

STORY DESIGN

PLOT & THE STRUCTURE TO SUPPORT IT
PLUS, CHAPTER BREAKS FOR NOVELS

PRESENTING YOUR STORY in a format the reader will recognize is crucial. Understanding how **Plot** and **Structure** work together in novels and scripts will help you craft your best effort and probably cut down on edits and rewrites.

Note: The diagrams included in this book can assist in your design.

Plot covers *content.* It is the series of events that happen in a story. These events are then divided into smaller segments called scenes. Scenes are purposed to elicit emotion by revealing characters' relationships, displaying their actions, and explaining what motivates them to take such action.

THE HEART OF ANY PLOT

- *Main Character/Hero/Protagonist:* Someone called to adventure.
- *Goal/Mission:* What he desperately wants.
- *Motivation/Incentive:* The reason he wants it.
- *Opposition/Conflict:* Obstacles that prevent him from effortlessly getting it.
- *Endgame:* His ultimate success or failure.

Structure covers *organization*. It involves crafting a timeline for the *content* and aligning events in a sequence that will make sense to the audience.

THE BASIS OF STRUCTURE

- **When** story events happen.
- **Where** story events happen.

Everything that happens to characters is positioned in a framework to occur at a strategic time and place. Best approach? Decide where and when a scene will deliver the most emotional impact. Decide where and when a scene will best push the plot toward resolution.

Common sense will help you figure out the proper order of events. Consider *cause and effect*. For instance, if you brush your teeth *after* you eat lunch rather than *before*, you'll have fresher breath all afternoon. If you study *before* your exam rather than *after*, you're more likely to get a better grade. If you put the bikes in the garage *before* a storm hits rather than *after*, you'll protect them from damage.

I know these are entry-level examples. But trust me, if you apply the simple logic to your characters' lives, that *their actions, smart or dumb, will trigger consequences*, you will develop an instinct for crafting a believable, commonsense timeline. Your scenes will fall smoothly in order like dominoes.

Storyboard

Post-it notes and index cards are useful for labeling and organizing scenes. You can see the bigger picture and move scenes around.

A WORD ABOUT CHAPTERS

READERS EXPECT CHAPTER BREAKS IN NOVELS

THE USE OF **CHAPTER BREAKS** divides your book into enjoyable, easy-to-follow sections. As established, a story (including a script) is a series of events broken down into scenes. A novel has a unique setup, with its scenes divided into *Chapters.* There are typically one to four scenes in a *Chapter.* If necessary, an extended scene can be broken into a few *Chapters.*

Such breaks are helpful when there is a shift in time, location, emotion, narrator, or any combination. A break allows you to leap forward in your plot without padded explanation and description. The reader is smart enough to bridge the gap in the action and adjust to any shifts you make.

A *Chapter* should begin with at least a small hook to stimulate curiosity. It can finish on a cliffhanger or resolution to an issue. There should be at least a slight feeling of closure by the *Chapter's* end.

The reader needs these breaks. It gives them a chance to take in your message before venturing forward to take in more. Or it can provide them a good stopping point for the day, a place to stuff their bookmark. The reader can confidently pick up the story without backtracking if done correctly.

CHAPTER BREAK EXAMPLE
AN EFFICIENT LEAP FORWARD

CHAPTER ONE

Ian stops short at the end of the old pier as the crooks thunder across its rickety planks in hot pursuit. He sees no option but to jump! Inhaling a gust of salty sea air and courage, Ian hits the surface of the moonlit water with a stinging bang and scuttles deeper into its dark, frigid depths. Sheer panic spurs him to swim away fast and hard.

CHAPTER TWO

Ian awakes in a dim, dank space, stretched out on a lumpy mattress. He is dressed in dry clothes and wrapped tight in a rough blanket that scratches his chin. Relief floods his system as he recognizes the sway of a boat's hull. One minute, he felt like a goner, and now—a second chance! Somebody has gone to the trouble of rescuing him. He blinks to discover a withered-looking man with a scruffy beard, smelling of sweat and tobacco, peering at him intently. "You've been out like a light for ten hours, son. Luckily for you, I could pull you aboard on my own. You were bobbing on the waves like a dead mackerel."

Chapter Two has leaped in time, location, and emotion. That's a lot of change. Yet the reader shouldn't feel cheated. It's easy to imagine the details of the rescue without a drawn-out play-by-play that would bog down the story. The plot jumps forward efficiently.

Essential Takeaway

You will learn where to insert **Chapter Breaks** by tracking the rise and fall of action in your scenes. You will also figure out how to spring forward between chapters, allowing the reader to fill in any blanks. It simply takes practice.

Note: We can learn about crafting clear **Chapter Breaks** from many mystery and suspense novels. They often have short chapters, each with a quick rise in action followed by a tense cliffhanger. This rapid seesaw technique keeps the reader curious and on edge.

THREE ACTS

COUNT ON IT!

STORIES COME IN VARIOUS FORMS beyond the novel, including short stories, illustrated children's books, graphic novels, stage plays, and screenplays. Genres range from mystery to romance to science fiction to horror and more. Some tales host a cast of thousands. Some boast as few as one, two, or three characters.

No matter the type of story or word count, a plot will be divided into three acts:

- BEGINNING
- MIDDLE
- END

This rule of thumb will aid you in crafting any tale, large or small.

In the next section, I present various diagrams to demonstrate the plotting process, ranging in complexity. Perhaps you want to stick with my **Basic Story Box** or **Basic Story Graph**, take **The Three-Act Journey**, or dive deeper with the detailed **Three-Act Story Arc**.

I've also included a Storyboard model for tracking scenes in advance and a Calendar illustration to precisely log when events happen.

Take note: You may prefer to digitally work with these kinds of diagrams. Every story you write will be its own unique adventure. Experiment to discover what methods bring out your best efforts.

Simplified Storytelling

The basic diagram for any plot.

STORY BOX

Beginning	• Who • What • Where • When	
Middle	• Problem	
End	• Solution	

Simplified Storytelling

The basic diagram for any plot.

STORY BOX

Beginning	• Who • What • Where • When	• John and Ryan. • Find a spaceship. • In their backyard. • At midnight.
Middle	• Problem	• Stranded Martians seek help to refuel their ship before dawn.
End	• Solution	• After a night of research, the boys provide a 2-liter bottle of Coke and a package of Mentos.

Basic Story Graph

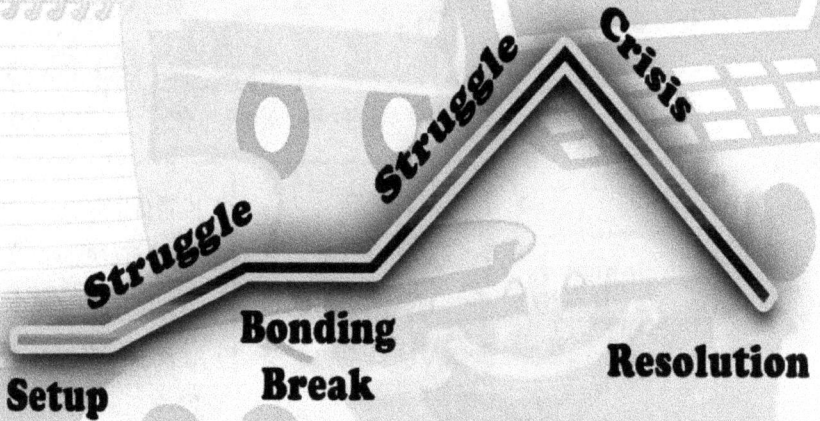

Struggle

Struggle

Crisis

Setup

Bonding
Break

Resolution

Setup: Main Character is Introduced in the Ordinary World

Struggle: A Problem Arises

Bonding Break: There is a Relief from Tension

Struggle: Trouble Increases

Crisis: Matters Worsen

Resolution: Problems are Resolved, Loose Ends Tied Up

Three-Act Journey

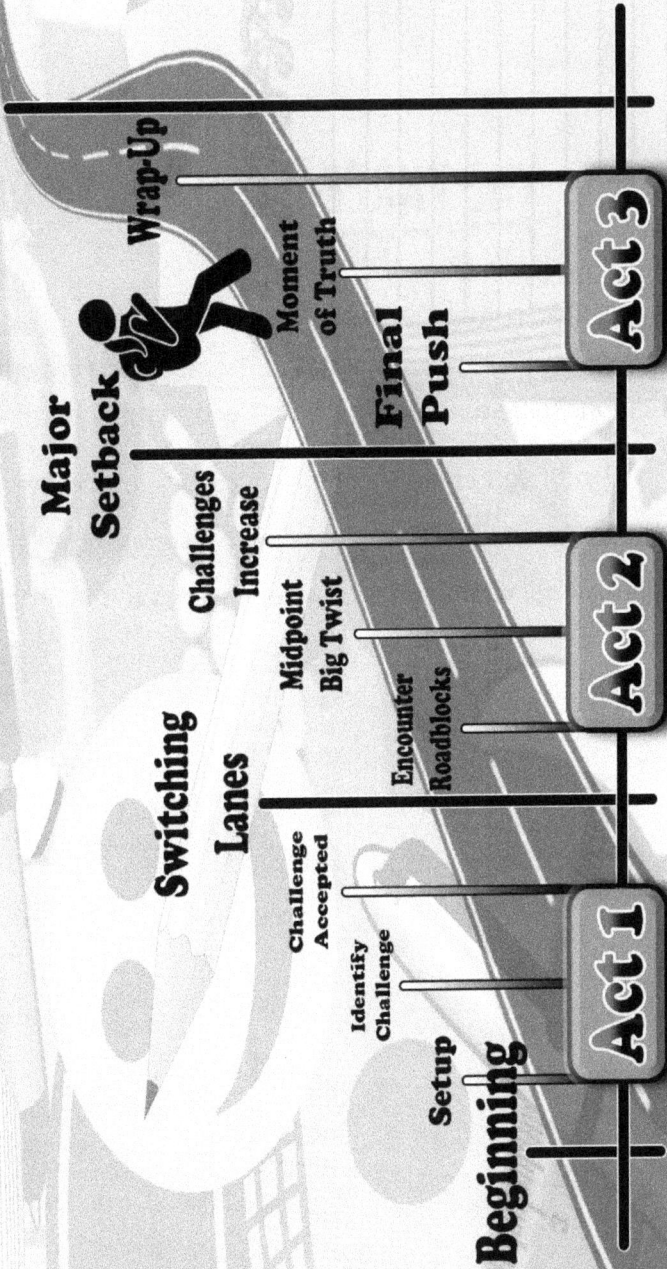

Beginning — **End**

Act 1
- Setup
- Identify Challenge
- Challenge Accepted

Act 2
- Switching Lanes
- Encounter Roadblocks
- Midpoint Big Twist
- Challenges Increase

Act 3
- Major Setback
- Final Push
- Moment of Truth
- Wrap-Up

THE THREE-ACT STORY ARC

THIS STRUCTURE IS MORE COMPLEX than the basic examples but still relatively easy to understand. The standards are only an approximation. Your story may not fit perfectly, and that's okay.

Tip: If you choose to plot your story in advance on a **Storyboard**, you may find my **Three-Act Story Arc** diagram a helpful guide. It will help you arrange your scenes in the proper Three-Act order.

ACT ONE

APPROXIMATELY 25% OF THE STORY

SETUP (Ordinary Girl In An Ordinary World)

This segment introduces the **Hero/Protagonist** in her **Ordinary World.** It is a platform to display her everyday interactions with other important characters. The idea is to provide a contrast to her **Special World** destination. The **Setup** should be strong enough to capture the reader's interest—include a hook—and tug at the audience's emotions by revealing the **Hero's** vulnerability/heart.

INCITING INCIDENT (Wakeup Call)

This segment provides a launchpad for the main event. A dramatic occurrence or opportunity arises that startles the **Hero** and challenges her comfort zone. Depending on your story's genre, word count, and target audience, this event could be large or small. However, a disruption caused by an **Antagonist/External Force** triggers some internal discomfort. She awakens to a new desire to switch things up.

CALL TO ADVENTURE (Humans Resist Change)

The **Hero** musters the courage to react to the incident/disruption at this turning point. A central goal/mission begins to materialize as she debates whether to risk her secure situation to pursue the new opportunity. She has second thoughts about leaving her comfort zone but eventually decides to answer the call to action. She ultimately launches into unfamiliar *Special World* territory and reacts to any early surprises. (The situation likely won't entirely be as she pictured it.) She will then be compelled to set a clear goal (decide what she's precisely after) and imagine a finish line in reaching that goal.

ACT TWO

MARCH ON! (Discomfort Zone Ahead)

The *Hero* pushes forward to reach her goal. She struggles to adapt to unforeseen obstacles as they unfold. She attempts to make wise choices. All choices, good and bad, have consequences. She will encounter setbacks. But she will also win a series of small victories to help retain her morale and keep the audience captivated enough to ask: *And then what happened?*

MIDPOINT (Point Of No Return)

The *Ordinary World* is officially in the rearview mirror as the *Hero* is gaining wisdom and reaching conclusions on her quest. However, a fresh twist/revelation turns the story in a new direction. Our girl is now stuck at the crossroads as she struggles with additional complications, and doubt creeps into her master plan. Fortuitously, these complications provide valuable life lessons that she can apply in the showdown in *Act Three.* Remember, as in life, the *Hero* must experience human growth through trial and error. Her perseverance pushes the plot forward.

THREAT INCREASES (Higher Stakes Stronger Setbacks)

The **Antagonist/External Force** recognizes the escalating strength and determination in the **Hero** and ramps up the opposition. The **Hero** feels the strain as she grapples with the fresh pressure surge.

ROCK BOTTOM (The Agony of Defeat)

External and **Internal Conflicts** crush the **Hero.** Her faith, optimism, and stamina are at an all-time low. Her original goal now seems like an impossible dream.

LET'S TWIST AGAIN (Sweet Inspiration)

A glimmer of inspiration sparks hope! This unexpected plot twist might come from the **Hero's** brilliant idea, assistance from a friend, such as a **Sidekick** or **Mentor**, a random lucky break, or another imaginative resource. What matters most is that she feels energized enough to make one last push out of her utter despair. (The audience will not begrudge a lucky break reasonable in size, as they have fully invested in her success by now.)

ACT THREE

APPROXIMATELY 25% OF THE STORY

IN IT TO WIN IT (Victory In Sight)

Reenergized, the *Hero* plots a new strategy requiring ingenuity and courage. She feels capable, having grown in wisdom and experience since leaving her *Ordinary World*. She has learned much about her adversary over time—specifically by *Midpoint*—and feels she can outwit them.

SHOWDOWN (The Big Push)

The moment of truth that the audience has been waiting for! The *Hero* steps up to face her adversary squarely and dramatically does battle to achieve her goal. Her issues are addressed and resolved here; her successes and failures are evaluated.

RESOLUTION (It's A Wrap)

The *Hero* is established in her *New Reality*. She may or may not have returned to her *Ordinary World*, but the journey has changed her circumstances forever. In chasing her goal, she has grown internally, which has likely caused external environmental changes. Closure is critical in this segment. The audience will appreciate that any loose ends between characters are tied up, their emotions dealt with, and their victories savored.

The most satisfying Endgame: The **Hero** and the audience have grown from lessons learned in the journey and are better for it.

Assignment

Fun way to familiarize yourself with the **Three-Act Story Arc**: Shift into editor mode as you read books and watch shows. Examine the story structure. You will soon learn to recognize where the acts start and stop. It is a formula. This exercise will help you in constructing your stories.

The Three-Act Story Arc

Act 1

Setup
Protagonist's Ordinary World

Inciting Incident
Launchpad to Main Event

The Three-Act Story Arc

Act 1

Call to Adventure

Turning Point Where Protagonist Chooses to Answer the Call and Launches into Unfamiliar Special World Territory

The Three-Act Story Arc

Act 2

Carry On

Protagonist Pushes Forward to Reach Goal.

Midpoint

Point of No Return. A Twist Complicates Matters.

The Three-Act Story Arc

Act 2

Threat Increases
Antagonist Ramps Up Opposition

Rock Bottom
Conflicts Crush the Protagonist

The Three-Act Story Arc

Act 2

Lets Twist Again

Positive Plot Twist that Energizes the Protagonist

The Three-Act Story Arc

Act 3

In It to Win It
Victory in Sight

Showdown
Protagonist Versus Antagonist

The Three-Act Story Arc

Act 3

Resolution

Loose Ends Are Tied Up Here

SUBPLOT

A MINI STORY WITH MEANING

PLOT: A series of events that unfold in your story in segments called scenes.

SUBPLOT: A series of smaller events that unfold in your story, co-existing with the Main Plot.

THE CHALLENGE IS TO WEAVE ALL EVENTS into a symmetrical *bigger picture*.

Visualize a hanging pot of ivy. How smaller vines sprout and intertwine with the main ones is a wonder of nature. Ultimately, all you see is the plant as a whole. **Subplots** should weave through a story with the same seamless result.

Are Subplots Necessary? No. Not all stories have subplots. Not all stories need them. It depends on word count, complexity, and the author's skill level.

Where Do Subplots Come From? Side stories may emerge as you storyboard the big picture. Or minor characters may trigger subplots later as you delve deeper into your storyline, inspiring you to toss them into small separate *situations* as their personalities take shape.

When cleverly used, these characters can effectively spark plot lulls and offer insight and enrichment to your **Special World.** Their actions can influence the struggles in the main storyline by offering comic relief or assistance or further complicating matters. Plus, **Subplots** provide another opportunity for the all-important **Bonding Break** scenes.

Subplots may or may not involve **Central Characters.** They may or may not connect directly to the **Main Plot.** However, the best **Subplots** relate to the core story and give the **Hero's** journey deeper meaning, as demonstrated in the following example.

SUBPLOT INCLUDED
YOU "BET"-CHA!

No-nonsense cop, Detective Shane, is pursuing a dangerous mobster. Meanwhile, his sneaky, carefree Grandpa Earl secretly runs an illegal gambling operation out of his nursing home to help residents pay their outrageously high fees. Shane's mobster hunt is the **Main Plot.** Grandpa's side hustle is the **Subplot.** Humor and tension ensue as Grandpa Earl conceals his deeds and treats his uptight, naïve grandson to the high life with some of his profits. Plots converge as the mobster tries to crush Grandpa's operation, and the detective must intercede. This story also works on a bonding level, drawing out the pair's communication problems and allowing them room to grow.

Structure Point: Subplots work best if they appear by **Midpoint in Act Two**, in a romantic relationship by the end of **Act One**.

Essential Takeaway

Like **Plots, Subplots** emerge from well-drawn characters, the circumstances they stumble into, the choices they make, and the consequences of those choices. Your audience must *care* enough about the bonus situation to invest in it.

No Subplot should ever feel forced. Such attempts become a nuisance to the reader. The author wasted time writing it, and the reader views it as a frustrating detour that *detracts* from the story. They skim pages to get back to the action.

Assignment

Go forth and study the **Subplots** in various novels. You will quickly learn to distinguish great additions from cumbersome ones. This exercise will help train you to spot plotting problems in your work.

SETTING

SPECIFY TIME AND LOCATION
CREATE A SENSE OF PLACE

ESTABLISHING A PROPER **SETTING** for each scene of your story is fundamental. You want to tell the audience when and where an event is happening quickly and plainly.

ARE THEY—
- Shopping in a grocery store at closing time?
- Playing early morning basketball in a gym?
- Sitting behind a desk in an office or a classroom during lunch?
- Walking down a country lane or a city street at dawn?
- Swimming in a lake at twilight?
- Hiding in a closet at midnight?
- Golfing on a course in the afternoon?

The goal is to create an environment the reader can relate to, interesting enough to lure them into the action. Not only must they *care* about the characters, but they should also want to jump *inside* the location with them.

Note the many components that can help you construct a vibrant sense of place for the reader.

SET THE SCENE
USEFUL PROP SUGGESTIONS

- **People**—Server/Doctor/Teacher/Friend/Enemy/Robber
- **Geography**—Suburbs/City/Country/Mountains/Lakeshore/Desert
- **Indoor/Outdoor**—Musty Basement/Cozy Kitchen/Ballfield/Farm
- **Day of the Week**—7 Amazing Choices
- **Time of Day**—Morning/Afternoon/Evening/Night
- **Season**—Fall/Winter/Spring/Summer/Specific Holiday
- **Century**—Past/Present/Future
- **Weather Conditions**—Sunny/Stormy/Snowy/Cloudy/Windy/Foggy
- **Smell**—Coffee/Grilled Meat/Lilacs/Garbage/Rain/Smoky/Fresh Air
- **Taste**—Sweet/Sour/Salty/Tangy
- **Sound**—Loud/Shrill/Silent/Echo
- **Feel/Sensation**—Hot/Cold/Sharp/Sticky/Slick/Damp

It is incredible how powerful such elements can be. It is up to you to decide how much detail you will add to your descriptions. Some writers use a lot of imagery, while others allow the reader to fill in the bigger picture with minimal prompts. You will find your balance as you write.

Assignment

Create brief scenes using some of the elements listed above. Note how quickly you can draw a vivid atmosphere with a few well-placed details. Also, investigate how your favorite authors create a sense of place.

Mark Your Calendar

A great way to track what happens on what day in your story is to log it on a calendar. Preferably in pencil to make changes easy. That way, you have the order of events at your fingertips as you write. You can buy a calendar or create one. I recommend using one with large boxes. You will fully appreciate its value once you start assigning days of the week to scenes.

Sunday	Monday	Tuesday	Wed	Thursday	Friday	Saturday

THE RISE AND FALL OF CONFLICT

SHAPE AND MANAGE SCENES BY LEVERING TENSION

I'VE DEMONSTRATED HOW THE **THREE-ACT-STRUCTURE** WORKS and how *Conflict* provides the necessary fuel to any story. Let's take a closer look at how to effectively lay out *Conflict* on a sliding scale of *Tension*, keeping the audience eager and on their toes.

Conflict generates *Tension* in humans. We all feel the strain in everyday life. There are tricks to producing the same anxiety in characters, with restful breaks in between.

STRETCH TENSION TO THE MAX WITH THE TAFFY PULL TRICK

In the "olden days," people made their taffy in a kettle on the stove. They would take the warm, gooey mixture off the heat and, before it could harden, would quickly pull the candy to suppleness. It stretched a long way without snapping. Oh, how delicious a piece of pulled taffy tastes!

Building *tension* in a scene works in much the same delicious way. You create an uncomfortable situation. Then you start the slow stretch and pull-pull-pull your characters into the thick of trouble.

Toss in **delays** and instill **hesitation** in your characters. This technique will create a sense of **anxiety and anticipation** in the audience.

Sometimes, the tension is high octane. Sometimes, it is low grade. In all cases, ramp up the urgency by **making them wait** for the payoff, at least a little while. Emotional fulfillment is always sweeter if the audience must first run up that hill with your protagonists and mimic their every huff and puff before enjoying the resolution you ultimately deliver.

All the tension threads running through your plot and any subplots should be easy to follow and escalate over time. By the story's end, you should provide a resolution for the separate threads. In other words, you should not leave any issues hanging unless you have a logical reason or plan a series. Then, you may imply that a future installment will hold solutions.

HOW TO PRODUCE THIS HULLABALOO

You ramp up the tension by putting characters **under pressure** as they pursue their goals. It is human nature to lose objectivity in an emotional squeeze and act out in spontaneous ways. These unforeseen responses are **plot twists** that surprise and delight the reader.

TENSION TRIGGERS

LET'S GET DESPERATE

DEADLINES

A preset endgame creates a state of urgency.

- He must complete the exam in two hours.
- The bakery holding their wedding cake closes at one o'clock.
- She must submit the scholarship application by midnight.
- The kidnappers demand the ransom be paid by tomorrow morning.
- The star witness must appear in court before the noon recess.
- Articles for the newspaper are due by Friday.

THE NEED FOR SPEED

Pump up the adrenaline. Put a character on the run for a large or small task, and everybody will breathlessly tag along.

- "Drive back to the shop. We can't serve celebrities the salad without croissants."
- "Quick! Mop up that grape juice before it stains Grandma's floor."

- "Turn on the siren, Sergeant. That van in the left lane was reported stolen!"
- "I see the finish line. Pedal faster!"
- "The open portal to our bedroom is shrinking! Run for it!"
- "Step on it, driver. The curtain rises in ten minutes, and I'm the star of the show!"

DELAYED MESSAGES
Oh, the agony of waiting it out.

- "Why won't he answer the phone?"
- "Please don't put me on hold again!"
- She intercepts the message slip and destroys it.
- He mistakenly tells the wrong brother.
- The mailman delivers the invitation to the wrong address.
- He misses her at the coffee shop by five minutes.

SUDDEN PANIC ATTACKS
Edgy, abrupt time crunches spike blood pressure.

- "A lady is drowning in the hotel pool! And I can't swim!"
- He crawls to the fire alarm as flames engulf the building.
- He gets lost delivering medicine to the gravely ill boy.
- Mall security searches for the wandering toddler.
- "Evacuate! A bomb is ticking in the cafeteria!"
- "That clock is slow. We have seconds before this vault seals shut for the night."

WITHHELD OR CONTRIVED AFFECTION
a/k/a PAINFUL HEART SQUEEZE

Everyone longs to be heard and appreciated. Nobody likes to be left out, rejected, or tricked. Universal injuries that people understand on impact—guaranteed.

- She yearns for her cold mother's approval.
- He refuses to acknowledge his stepchildren.
- She secretly disinherits the grandson who helped her the most.
- The gang sneaks to the movies without him.
- His birth mother refuses to acknowledge him in public.
- She dates him briefly for his generous gifts.

DANGER
Bring on the shivers.

- A garbage can clatters halfway down the dark, deserted alley.
- The jolly Santa is concealing a pistol.
- "I think she poisoned our soup."
- "Hello? Police? A car has been tailing me for miles."
- There are fresh footprints in the snow leading to the shed.
- They arrive home to find their garage door open.

WRONGLY ACCUSED

An injustice sparks indignation.

- The college dean expels a student for cheating.
- A supervisor accuses a bookkeeper of fraud.
- A doctor blames a nurse for a patient overdose.
- A judge charges a lawyer with jury tampering.
- A wife alleges her husband was unfaithful.
- The parent punishes the wrong child for the broken lamp.

THE CHILL-OUT

IT'S TIME FOR INTERMISSION!

WHILE **TENSION** THROUGHOUT A STORY is necessary to hold the audience's attention, not all scenes should be supersized struggles. In other words, not every scene must be, or should be, rife with **Conflict.**

As in life, the audience requires regular breaks from stress in your Special World.

The trick is to add low-impact scenes that still have purpose and will move the story forward. I call them ***Bonding Breaks or a Relaxation Pause.***

Bonding Breaks are a place to offer the audience comfort in real-time, expose vulnerabilities, and suggest *hope* for optimistic resolutions to the mounting tensions.

It is a space to explore relationships between characters and reveal their personalities through conversation and interaction. It is a cozy place to express feelings and share secrets and ambitions. It is an opportunity to introduce friends and family to one another and the audience in a non-threatening atmosphere. Or use the scenes to provide helpful background info, including where and how the characters work and live.

BONDING SETTINGS
Safe havens for relaxation and play.

- A sporting event.
- A restaurant or picnic.
- A movie or theater date.
- A simple home-cooked meal.
- An amusement park or fair.
- A party invitation.
- A card or bingo game.
- A walk in the park.
- A car, train, or bus ride.
- A garden.
- A midnight conversation at the kitchen table.
- A coffee date.

MAXIMIZE BONDING SCENES

REVEAL TRUE CHARACTER WITH SMALL PLOT DEVICES

GLIMPSES OF VULNERABILITY
- The crabby waitress sneaks some children a complimentary slice of pie.
- A family pretends to enjoy their beloved aunt's gooey chicken ala king.
- The strict librarian reads to the lonely girl.
- The uptight socialite botches mini golf.
- The strict Dad chooses to comfort the daughter who broke curfew.
- The strict principal agrees to sit in the dunk tank at the school carnival.
- The tough private eye wrangles a crying baby.

THAT'S NOT TO SAY THE SCENES SHOULD NECESSARILY BE SERIOUS. Not at all! Laughter is most welcome in a **Bonding Break**. And you don't have to be a standup comic to accomplish a light touch. For an easy fix, reveal a character's shortcoming, eccentricity, or simple mistake to spark fun. Or create an illogical response to some predictable behavior. Think *awkward* moment; devise an interaction that will cause minor discomfort to someone and cause a chuckle.

TOUCHES OF HUMOR

- The dithering granny fleeces the guys at poker.
- The chef is so nervous on a date that he burns a simple meatloaf.
- A toddler abruptly reveals his uncle's secret love of cheesy romcoms.
- A guy mixes up two gifts and, in horror, must watch the dual unwrapping.
- The best friend reveals a girl's secret crush to the secret crush.
- The oblivious aunt repeats the same stories.
- The pompous waiter acts like he owns the place.
- The girl refuses to order lunch and steals from her friends' meals.

Essential Takeaway

If you can swing it, always mine deep for emotion in these moments.

DIALOGUE

ANY WORDS SAID BY ANY
CHARACTER TO ANYONE

CONVERSATIONS BETWEEN **FICTIONAL CHARACTERS** are a step up from commonplace real-life chatter. *Enhanced Characters* speak *Enhanced Dialogue* in the *Special World.*

SPOKEN WORDS = PURPOSE!

Carefully craft each conversation with a specific purpose in mind.

Get the point across as economically as possible: Strive to express a maximum amount of info in the fewest possible words.

If a character is rambling on, there should be a reason. Perhaps there is no other way to convey important information. Or the speaker is stalling for time, hiding a secret, or simply the nervous type.

DIALOGUE RUNS ALONG THREE DISTINCT TRACKS

Said To Others:

"Bella will meet us at the movie theater."

Said To Self:

"I should've kept my mouth shut."

Said To Reader/Audience:

"My story begins on the first day of last summer."

DIALOGUE SHOULD ACCOMPLISH AT LEAST ONE OF THREE TASKS

Provide revealing information to the audience: (Lucky and wealthy)

"It's Henry's twenty-first birthday. His dad bought him another Rolex."

Move the plot forward: (Unlucky, forced to address change)

"You are fired, Jason! Pack up your gear and leave."

Define a character through a unique perspective: (Superstitious)

"*You* broke that mirror, Annika? You can expect seven years of bad luck!"

THE ART OF CONVERSATION = PRACTICE!

Writing **Dialogue** is an ability that does not come naturally to all writers. But you can learn how to make your conversations sparkle.

Study plays, novels, and shows with new awareness. Note how smoothly good conversations reveal character and move the plot along. Note how boring or useless **Dialogue** slows the story and sometimes confuses the scene.

Listen to **Real World** conversations with the finely tuned ear of a student learning a new language. Evaluate the teller's intention and its impact on the receiver. Eavesdrop everywhere. You will soon note that people are blabbing in the supermarket checkout line, on the bus, and at the coffee shop. Oh, so many intriguing conversations take place at the coffee shop. For some strange reason, people often speak confidentially to one another there, as if in the privacy of their own kitchen.

The topics of public discussion are limitless. Secrets, theories, accusations, and suspicions pour out in unstructured sentences, abbreviated words, and slang. Voices ring out in fear, anger, joy, and passion. You may even pick up a plot idea or two.

Luckily for us, all the world is a stage. And people love to sing out and be noticed.

And it's not just *what* people say that is important, but *how* they say it. A person's *tone* sometimes reveals as much or more about their true feelings. Consider that supermarket checkout line. The young mother denies her son's request for a candy bar with a serenity that doesn't gel with the hardness of her eyes. The older man buys a bottle of cough syrup and wishes the cashier a nice day in a scary, coarsened voice. The teenage girl giggles into her phone as she recounts someone tripping down the school stairs. In all cases, there is more than meets the *tone*. There is underlying impatience, an illness, and mean-spiritedness, respectively.

THE CLARITY AND PURPOSE OF DIALOGUE

A company picnic is supposed to be the subject. Study the following examples for clarity and content.

A WASTE OF SPACE

"It looks like rain, Tess."

"Is rain in the forecast, Ben?"

"Not sure."

"With any luck, it will hold off."

"Yes, with any luck, it will."

This exchange reveals absolutely nothing significant about the characters or plot. Tess and Ben are discussing the threat of rain, but there is no indication when it is coming or why it would pose a problem. Also, the pair expresses no emotional vibe to help define their relationship. It's hard to invest in such one-dimensional characters or the state of the weather.

RUNAWAY TRAIN TALK

"Tess, have you seen next Saturday's forecast? Looks like rain could spoil our company picnic!"

"Oh, Benny Ben, you got the lousy creamer for the breakroom again. Everyone hates the powdered stuff."

"*You* hate the powdered stuff. The boss heaps it into his coffee. Now, about the company picnic. We haven't even discussed our menu."

"Well, if it's gonna rain, what's the use? Have you seen Abby's hair today? What a bird's nest."

"Hey, my mom wears her hair like that."

"No, she doesn't. Can you please return the yucky creamer to the store and bring back the real deal?"

This conversation veers way off the rails. On the plus side, it is now clear why the weather is critical to Tess and Ben: they've scheduled a company picnic for Saturday. Through banter over creamer and bird's nest hair, it's evident that Tess and Ben share a comfortable relationship. But the topic of the scene is the picnic. The conversation should mainly focus on that.

PURPOSEFUL PROSE

"Tess, have you seen next Saturday's forecast? Looks like rain could spoil our company picnic!"

"Oh, Benny, Ben, say it ain't so. We have the event all planned. I sent the caterer a deposit this morning."

"I suppose we can plan to eat under the shelter of the pavilion, but the volleyball tournament on the beach could prove to be a washout."

"Maybe we can schedule the games around any waterworks."

"You're a brilliant woman. We'll continue to watch the forecast and rewrite our itinerary if necessary. Hey, let me pour you a coffee before you go."

"No thanks. I see you bought that yucky powdered creamer again."

"The boss loves it. Always happy to please him."

"Yeah, yeah. I hope that goofy grin freezes on your face one day."

This final conversation drives the plot because it squarely addresses the picnic and the threat of rain. Tess and Ben communicate with ease, suggesting they are accustomed to brainstorming. The creamer exchange, saved for the end this time, implies they are friendly enough to tease each other.

Plus, this version has a Basic Story Arc.

What: Employees are hosting a company picnic.

Problem: Rain threatens to spoil the volleyball tournament.

Solution: Check the forecast for the driest part of the day to host volleyball.

LOOK WHO'S TALKING

IN NOVEL FORM

A READER MUST ALWAYS BE AWARE OF WHO IS TALKING. The key to success is correctly punctuating, tagging, and arranging your *Dialogue* on the printed page as he expects and understands.

If you make significant grammatical errors, it will cause the reader to pause midstream in even the most captivating conversation and leap out of your *Special World* to take note of the *Real World* mistake. Even worse, it may cause him to confuse characters or plot points.

If you are unfamiliar with *Dialogue* formatting, there are many grammar resources to help. Meanwhile, here are a few basic guidelines.

TERMS

LABELS: The words added to *Dialogue* to identify who the speaker is and sometimes who the listener is, too. There are three popular options.

1. **Attach a Dialogue Tag:** The most common tag examples are: **he said, she asked, he added, she replied.** As you study popular fiction, you will note the use of these tags and many others: **murmured, shouted,** or **grumbled,** to name a few.

   Notice the shift in emotion with the use of different Tags. It is a commonly used shortcut that can help you quickly set the tone.

   "Watch your step," he said.
   "Watch your step," she whispered.
   "Watch your step!" she cried.
   "Watch your step," he begged.

2. **Insert a name in the Dialogue with or without a Tag:**

   "Violet, please come straight home after lunch," Mom said.
   "Violet, please come straight home after lunch."

3. **Connect a name with an Action Tag:**

   Isabel jiggled the doorknob. "Believe it or not, we're locked out of the office."

QUOTES: Quotation marks should bracket anything anyone says. Note that punctuation also goes *inside* the quotation marks.

TIPS

A Dialogue Tag follows the use of a comma.

"The baseball game is tomorrow," Ann said.

However, a Dialogue Tag, such as Ann said, never follows the use of a period.

"The baseball game is tomorrow."

A Dialogue Tag may or may not follow a question mark.

"Is the baseball game tomorrow?" John asked.
"Is the baseball game tomorrow?"

A Dialogue Tag may or may not follow an exclamation point.

"The baseball game is tomorrow!" John exclaimed.
"The baseball game is tomorrow!"

An Action Tag can efficiently identify the speaker and the listener.

Ann gave John a thumbs-up. "Yes, the baseball game is tomorrow."

A name can be inserted in a sentence to only identify the listener.

"The baseball game is tomorrow, John."

DIVISION

Split a conversation into paragraphs, with one speaker per paragraph. When a new character speaks, start a new paragraph. Never include the speech of two characters in a single paragraph.

- Cathy peeked into the bedroom. "Did you send Spencer to the hardware store for more paint, Dan?"
- "Yes. You'll be happy to hear I also asked Spence to stop for Chinese takeout on his way home."

Sometimes, when a character has much to say, dividing her speech into multiple paragraphs simplifies her message. When you split the Dialogue into paragraphs, omit the quotation mark at the end of subsequent paragraphs. However, one last quotation mark is necessary to close off the end of her speech.

- "I made all the arrangements for our trip. We'll take the first flight out on Friday and arrive in Chicago around ten.
- "Aunt Joan is planning a large lunch for us and invited what seems like half our family tree!
- "Hannah has agreed to pick us up at the airport. She'll drive us directly to Aunt Joan's apartment."

You'll get the hang of Dialogue basics in no time!

SHOW AND TELL

SHOWING ROCKS!
BUT TELLING ISN'T ALWAYS TERRIBLE

SHOW DON'T TELL IS A STANDARD WRITER'S RULE. Why? The **Show** technique pulls the reader into a character's shoes most effectively. The reader feels he is *sharing* an event versus merely *receiving* a narrator's version, which invites him to draw his own conclusions versus being told what to think.

There is wisdom behind this rule, but it isn't the whole story.

A BASIC COMPARISON OF THE TWO METHODS:

Showing: A writer's use of action and dialogue to take hold of a reader's emotions and draw him into a situation for a *firsthand* experience.

An appeal to any of the reader's five senses will help lure him in.

Telling: A *secondhand* report supplied by the narrator, designed to relay necessary information to the reader.

Novels require some **Telling** in them. And sometimes that can be the better choice.

Let's explore both techniques.

SHOW VERSUS TELL

TWO VERSIONS OF THE SAME SCENARIO
A POWER-OF-SHOWING DEMO

Telling: Remote Bystander Mode

Luke Hayden's teacher accused him of cheating on the final exam. He hadn't done it, but Professor Simpson was too narrowminded to consider Luke's side of the story. He tried to explain his predicament to the educator, that he'd brought his phone into the classroom because his grandma's condition had suddenly worsened at the hospital. But there was nothing for it. Even though he'd gotten a perfect score, Luke felt destined to flunk the course.

Showing: Invested Participant Mode

"Hayden! Front and center!"

Luke Hayden flinched at the rear of the classroom, where he'd lingered to stuff his belongings into his backpack. Most students were rushing to the exit like the place was on fire. Everyone knew Professor Simpson's nasty growl was as bad as his bite, and nobody wanted to be next in his line of fire. Today's final exam had been especially brutal. Fingers trembled over keypads as students wrestled with tricky multiple-choice questions.

Luke's gut painfully twisted as reality set in. Simpson must have spotted his forbidden phone.

"Hayden!"

Luke bounded up the aisle to the teacher's podium. "Sir, if I can explain—"

"You're a cheat," Simpson seethed. "And cheaters are out."

"My phone pinged, that's all."

"I'm not blind—or a fool!"

"Okay, I glanced at the screen. My grandma's been in the hospital all week after a stroke. She got worse overnight." Luke choked back a sob. "Mom says it doesn't look good..."

Simpson's brows arched over beady eyes. "No exception to my rules. Ever."

"But I'm innocent. *Please*—"

"Furthermore, I just had a quick look at your test results."

Luke blinked back tears. "Believe me, I studied hard."

"That's the thing, you got a perfect score."

"I did?"

"And it's so unlike you, Hayden."

"I swear to you, I earned it—to make Grandma proud."

"Fat chance. You're done."

The Show version better brings this edgy scene to life. Leaping into the action with Luke, sharing his pain and frustration firsthand versus learning of it secondhand, makes for entertaining drama. The reader is more likely to ask: *And then what happened?*

Now, sometimes, it is more advantageous to *Tell*. There are situations where, for instance, you efficiently want to account for a character's location or motivation, bridge gaps in the action, move the plot along economically, or report on the weather or time of day.

THE POWER OF TELLING
EFFICIENT MESSAGE DELIVERY

DEREK WENT TO THE STORE FOR GROCERIES, only to return thirty minutes later to discover his brother had taken off with his girl-friend.

Tim cut the grass and trimmed the hedges before the storm rolled in.

Phil had a restless night, so tiredly trudged through morning activities.

Ally drove the kids to school and then spent the day in a coffee shop writing an article.

Wesley debated whether to pick and choose his guests but ultimately invited the whole team to the party.

Mitch was delighted that Zoe spent the morning cleaning out the garage and treated her to lunch.

The Realtor showed Charles and Juliet twenty houses over several weeks before they settled on one.

Matt did two loads of laundry before he hit the gym.

Rob was sorry to miss most of the dinner party. There was a twisty detour through downtown due to roadwork, and he stopped to help a lady fix a flat tire.

After several clumsy attempts, Bethany managed to bake a cake for the fundraiser.

The city council meeting collapsed after two hours without approving a teacher pay raise or establishing a curfew ordinance.

Assignment

Notice writers' choices of **Show and Tell** in various genres. Are they effective? Would you have done some scenes differently?

TRUE IDENTITY—FALSE IDENTITY

OUR DOUBLE IDENTITY
UNDERSTANDING THE UNIVERSAL
HUMAN STRUGGLE

THE REAL WORLD IS A TOUGH PLACE TO NAVIGATE. Daily life can take its toll. None of us can escape suffering pain and disappointment at some point in our lives.

It is no wonder that we build a protective shell around our innermost selves, creating a **False/Imposter Identity,** as it were, to camouflage and protect our sensitive *True/Secret Identity.*

Think back, as recently as yesterday, to all the times, for one reason or another, you concealed your true feelings. People often rely on a standard of privacy and protection to survive.

If you've never considered that we habitually wear a **Mask** to hide our genuine and fragile selves, imagine what it would be like if you revealed everything that popped to mind as you went about your routine. We are estimated to make 35,000 decisions daily and process spontaneous surges of raw emotion. Yikes! How awful to be wholly on display as we explore options (engage in *Internal*

Conflict), all the while feeling vulnerable to possible ridicule and misinterpretation at every turn.

So, we habitually cherry-pick what we want to share of our genuine selves and with whom we want to share it. It's all about faith in our beliefs and trust in being understood and accepted by those we care about. That's a lifestyle of *healthy risk,* choosing to connect with those who matter most to us.

It is also healthy to do some truth-sharing from within. Consider that we sometimes lie to ourselves about our True Identity because self-examination can be especially painful.

Relying solely on a fake, challenge-free persona can seem attractive on the surface but makes for a shallow existence. While a thick shell can offer protection from the most vigorous emotional assaults, it can also keep a person stuck with **no opportunity for growth.**

Essential Takeaway

Personal growth cannot happen without *risk*. And *risk* involves revealing one's Secret Identity when the stakes are worth it.

Delegating this human challenge to your **Hero** in his **Special World** makes for a compelling story.

TRUE IDENTITY—FALSE IDENTITY

A CHARACTER'S DOUBLE IDENTITY
STORYBOOK HEROES MUST STRUGGLE TOO

STANDARD STORYTELLING PROCEDURE: To complete his mission, the **Hero** must summon the courage to step out of his **False/ Imposter Identity** and reveal his essential self, his **True/Secret Identity,** to get the job done. He will struggle internally (suffer Internal Conflict) and make tough choices.

In the **Setup,** we find our **Hero** stuck, feeling vulnerable due to some emotional setback. He may well think he has worked through his issues but hasn't, as he is presenting a **False Identity** to the world for self-protection.

Then, a life twist offers an intriguing, perhaps urgent, opportunity or goal. Pursuing this goal introduces a *risk* factor to the status quo. (Note that adding an element of risk to any character's goal gives them the depth and complexity necessary to capture audience interest.) The audience will be reluctant to invest in a dilemma if the risk is too low.

Under Pressure. The sudden pressure this risk generates drives the *Hero's essence* to the surface. He must choose: Dive back into his comfortable shell or tap into his *True Identity* for the strength to bravely pursue his new desire. Once he decides to move forward, more choices must follow, and those choices will generate consequences. Remember, *Choice/Consequence* is the energy that propels the *Hero* forward.

Numerous characters in your story may feel pressure points along the way, generating large or small choices. In every case, they should reveal at least a trace of *True Identity.*

TRUE IDENTITY

NOT ALWAYS PRETTY IN THE PRESSURE COOKER

RISK LAUNCHES **PROTAGONISTS** ON A JOURNEY OF DISCOVERY. For Villains, however, risk embarks them on a path of disintegration. Check out these mini-risks. Also, note how much these reveals use *Showing* versus *Telling* effectively.

HEROES IN THE MAKING
PROTAGONIST VERSION

Teagan entered the carnival midway with her two young children, Jack and Audrey, in hand. Music filled the air, along with the delicious smells of sweet cotton candy and savory fried foods. A Ferris wheel turned against the dark, starry sky. Cars zipped down a twisty roller coaster track. A carousel boasting colorful ponies whirled round and round.

Unfortunately, Teagan couldn't afford even one spin on the carousel for the kids. She was so short on cash due to car repairs that she'd been reluctant to bring them here. But as they had been so good all week, she couldn't deny them the pleasure of the carnival experience.

She had precisely five dollars and easily spent it on two ice cream cones and a lemonade to share.

They lingered on a hillside to watch the closing fireworks, then moved through the crowd toward the entrance. As Teagan paused at the curb to tie her son's shoe, she noted a well-dressed couple toting souvenirs rising from a nearby bench. Out of the man's pocket fell a twenty-dollar bill. She sucked in a breath of indecision as it fluttered out of sight under the wooden seat. The money would handily pay for some basics at the grocery store tomorrow. Dare she snatch it up? The gentleman likely wouldn't even miss it. Just as she was about to spring for the bill, five-year-old Audrey scrambled over to grab it. She proudly brought it to her mother, singing, "Finders Keepers!" Teagan shook her head. It was one thing to take it herself sneakily, but to allow her daughter to be a party to the theft was too large an ethical price to pay. "Sir!" she called out. "You lost something!"

Madison was fidgeting with excitement. Her eighth-grade Oakland Middle School class was off to explore the Natural History Museum, an hour away by bus. Madison had no interest in natural history, but the class's most popular girl, Tiffany, was taking an interest in her. Tiffany's lifelong BFF recently moved to Ohio, and Tiffany had been shopping for a suitable replacement, auditioning several girls before scoping out Madison. The winner would wear a charm bracelet identical to Tiffany's, crafted by her jeweler father. Things had been going well between the pair. Madison had done much to impress, getting a similar haircut, trendier clothing, and supplying treats from her aunt's bakery. Madison sensed this long bus ride might be the final test for approval. Tiffany was wearing two charm bracelets on her wrist—a sign that she might present one to her new BFF!

It was common practice for Tiffany to mock perceived flaws in people. Anyone with braces, chubby thighs, poor fashion sense, or bad hair was fair game. The last person to board the bus was Madison's neighbor, chaperone Mrs. Wilson. She was an awkward, heavyset woman who often volunteered at school because she had no family of her own.

As the packed bus edged into traffic, Mrs. Wilson was left with no seat and forced to stand in the aisle. Tiffany wasted no time in launching a full-scale whisper attack on the woman. Madison, admittedly, found some of the jokes funny. But deep down, her heart broke for her gentle neighbor, clinging to a pole for dear life as the bus lurched and swayed. Her stubby legs shook, her breathing got heavier, and her face grew tomato red. Finally, Madison could bear it no longer. Tearing her gaze away from the charm bracelet prize, she popped up from her seat and offered it to Mrs. Wilson. As Mrs. Wilson gratefully plopped down with Tiffany, wafting body odor, Madison bravely met Tiffany's glare with a defiant chin wobble. Tiffany angrily pocketed the extra charm bracelet, signifying the BFF audition was over. Madison surprised herself by being okay with that.

CHILLIN' FOR A VILLAIN

ANTAGONIST VERSION

WHILE SOME CHARACTERS WEAR **FALSE IDENTITIES** for protection, others wear them to control and exploit others. And there we have a strong catalyst for drama!

Gladys awoke to the barking of a dog. She climbed out of bed and peered out her kitchen window to confirm that, again, it was the Warner family's mongrel, Lucky, sniffing around her backyard bushes. How inconsiderate a breach of manners when the other neighbors kept their mutts in check. How inconvenient a conundrum for the street's beloved granny who routinely dished out delicious beverages and homemade pies in her spotless kitchen, along with subtle maneuvers to keep the neighborhood orderly.

She'd done her best to involve Amelia next door in the "mutt mess," repeatedly pressing *her* to report Lucky for the good of the street. But Amelia was either too stubborn or stupid to take proper direction and had done nothing about the dog. Well, this city code infraction had to stop—today! Gladys picked up her landline phone and punched in the proper digits to block her identity. Then she dialed City Hall, a number she'd committed to memory due to its usefulness in such matters of civic duty. "This is Amelia Olson of 974 Elmhurst Street," Gladys mimicked convincingly. "I'd like to report my neighbor's dog on the loose. The name of the owner is Warner, of 969 Elmhurst Street."

Gladys raked the same patch of leaves for an hour before finally spotting a uniformed animal control worker next door at Amelia's. Amelia's confused protests over the alleged complaint the city had received quickly drifted across the property line. The worker soon caught sight of Lucky and sprinted off to collect him and return him to the Warner house across the street.

Mission accomplished, Gladys silently crowed, meekly nodding at a bewildered Amelia before sauntering into her garage. It was high time she changed clothes and washed her hands. Jill Warner was coming to coffee momentarily and would no doubt need consolation over their tattletale neighbor and the hefty pet violation fine undoubtedly issued to her.

Wade believed most people were horrible drivers. They slowed down for yellow lights instead of speeding up. They hesitated at four-way stops. They often tapped their brake lights when Wade roared up behind them on the freeway. Bunch of morons!

Bad things always seemed to happen when he was in a hurry— like today! First, a delivery van had half-blocked his driveway for several long minutes. Then he'd been delayed by a Buick going ten miles under the speed limit on Route 61—the driver proved to be a frightened teenager. Hah! She'd better get accustomed to handling car horns.

As he wheeled into the strip mall parking lot, an elderly lady drifted into his path as she tried to navigate her heavy cart in the crosswalk. Who turned *her* loose on an unsuspecting world? Fury caused him to cut short as he wheeled his pickup into the last open space. Smash! The sturdy fender of his truck crushed the vintage Volkswagen Beetle like an eggshell. And what about that Volkswagen? It was within the yellow lines but not perfectly centered. He would leave a note with contact info if it had been his fault, which it wasn't. What must a guy do to catch a break in this world? At least this strip of vintage shops had no security cameras. He swiftly reversed to remove himself from the accident. The clock was ticking. He would have to find another specialty market—fast!

Twenty minutes later, Wade trotted into the lobby of radio station WBDX with a lavish bouquet of roses and gourmet goodies purchased on the station's credit card. The second shift crew cheered his arrival. He graciously thrust the goodie sacks at the grateful receptionist, then kissed the matronly station manager on the cheek as he presented her with the bouquet. "Happy Birthday, Joan!" he intoned melodiously. "From all of us!"

Leaving the blushing birthday girl who held the key to his promotion in his wake, he hurried to the control booth, donned a headset, and murmured his standard greeting into the microphone. "Good afternoon, loyal listeners. Doctor Russell, Tender Talk Therapist, is here to take your calls and ease your troubles…"

Assignment

Fast forward six months. Imagine where each character is now and write a scene about them.

Reminder: Actions, good or bad, eventually trigger justified consequences. It is reasonable that the Protagonists will continue to generate goodwill and experience personal growth, while the Antagonists, determined to exploit others for personal gain, will disintegrate in mind and spirit.

GAME OF NAMES

A WELL-TOLD STORY BENEFITS from choosing a thoughtful name for each character. The process can be fun.

You can elevate your reader's pleasure by making it easy to keep characters straight throughout the journey. It can be jarring to pause mid-page, unable to distinguish one character from another.

KEEP NAMES DISSIMILAR

Choosing distinctive names in the same manner as we choose various eye colors, hairstyles, and mannerisms can help to expertly brand characters' personalities and make them memorable to the reader.

While similar-looking names are common among our daily contacts in the *Real World,* we have the power to make them unique in our *Special World.*

Sometimes, it is helpful to link two characters by giving them first names that begin with the same letter if they are, for instance, related or dating. But generally speaking, choosing character first names that start with the same letter and especially have one syllable, such as Will, Wynn, and Wayne, can confuse the reader.

Names with the same look and cadence, such as Amanda, Amelia, and Andrea, or Donny, Danny, Davy, and Denny, also can be confusing.

Note how individual names pop when they vary in spelling, sound, and the number of syllables. A reader is less likely to confuse a Jake with an Andrew or a Riley.

You may argue that many fictional works have similar character names. I've noticed! Maybe it is done to add a touch of realism; perhaps the authors don't give it a second thought. The choice is entirely up to you. I always try to make my reader's experience as straightforward and rewarding as possible, and thoughtfully chosen names help.

THE NAME SEARCH

The Internet is a go-to for names. However, there are other creative ways to explore the name game. Over the years, I have collected names from phone directories, baby name books, newspapers, magazines, yearbooks, and children's programs for choir and orchestra concerts, dance recitals, and plays. Many such resources are a goldmine of unique first and last names. And what a bonus to find lyrical first and last name combos, thoughtfully invented by doting parents striving for the imaginative. I also note intriguing street names and link them together. Keep a notebook handy to record possibilities.

SHOW FOLK

Great names also come out of Hollywood. And not just from actors. Watch the credits roll at the end of movies and TV shows. There are great fictional names and cool, true-life names of directors, producers, writers, and technicians who make up the crew. There are so many options to mix and match.

DESCRIPTIVE CHARACTER NAMES

Another way to help your readers recognize a particular character is to give them a name or nickname that describes them.

Blade or Spike: Dangerous

Brick: Giant

Lily or Willow: Fragile

Ivory: Pale complexion

Azure or Indigo: Blue-streaked hair

Wheels: Owns a cool car

Slim: Skinny

Einstein: Smart

USEFUL TITLES

You can assign an authority figure or relative a respectful or affectionate title to define and individualize them.

Mrs. Cartwright

Mr. Bailey

Miss Jenson

Ms. Fowler

Sergeant Thorne

Congressman Leonard

Father Burnside

Professor Mason

Doctor Hadley

Principal Smithers

Reverend Darby

Aunt Elaine

Uncle Rick

Grandpa, Papa, Pop

Grandma, Gran, Gram, Nana

AGE-APPROPRIATE NAMES

Names, like clothing, come in and out of fashion. However, you can research some of the earlier mentioned resources to track down the trendiest names of a decade. You will find some very specific to a generation, which will help classify your character's age.

ASSEMBLING A CAST OF CHARACTERS

PUTTING YOUR RESEARCH TO WORK

A HELPFUL BEGINNING IS TO TAKE A BLANK SHEET of paper and write down some potential names you've collected from your research. Then, link possible first and last names.

Next, fill in possible names following **Character Titles** using your personalized version of this book's blank **Cast of Characters Worksheet.** If you have more than one promising name for a character, no problem; list it. Now, study and compare your selections with an eye for individuality. It can take time to label your cast and decide what feels right. I approach it as a puzzle. Expect to shift the names around to get the right balance.

Note: A first name alone will often occur to you when shaping a character. And for the time being, it is enough. When introduced to someone in the Real World, we frequently feel a spark of connection at the first name stage. The bonding process is the same in fiction.

DEATH BACK TO LIFE—NOT ZOMBIES!

A JOURNEY OF REDEMPTION

Deliberately shattering a relationship to reconstruct it can be a rich source of tension in your story.

OUR CENTRAL STORYTELLING THEME is that humans long to connect emotionally with one another. Often, things go wrong when people don't measure up. Relationships break when forgiveness and understanding seem too high a price to pay.

These estrangement opportunities, catalysts for drama, can originate in your plot or be part of your backstory and be explained along the way.

An estrangement can play a major or a minor role in your storyline.

An audience instinctively relates to the pain of a broken "dead" relationship and will experience deep gratification in living through its renewal.

An emotionally frozen character on a slow thaw is showbiz at its best.

MJ'S HURT-TO-HOPE-TO-HEAL ROTATION

Hurt: Establish the rift. Even small devices work. Imagine someone crossing the street to avoid an interaction, glancing at Caller ID only to hit the phone's mute button, throwing an unopened letter into the fireplace, or speaking unkindly about someone. The audience wants to know why!

Hope: Chart the path to a second chance. The trick is to gradually tug at the audience's heartstrings as you urge them through your plotline. Make them yearn for characters to reconnect. You want the audience to feel the pain of loss down to their toes, to take up the cause passionately. Perhaps it is a brother/sister rift or a broader family rift. Maybe lovers or best friends are estranged.

Maybe only one party is big enough to make the first move, or the desire to reconnect is mutual. Possibly, only a third party sees the wisdom of their rejoining—at first.

These divisions can be due to a misunderstanding, a cruel argument, a secret, a difference in moral code, an accident, or a heat-of-the-moment betrayal. And the fallout characters are living with can run the dramatic spectrum, from abandonment, rejection, physical injury, poverty, or even death.

You may have a chosen character to root for. But as in real life, there are two sides to every story, so try to offer at least a little insight into opposing positions through action, dialogue, or—if using multiple points of view, the internal reflection of interested parties.

The struggle toward renewal, the yearning for reconciliation and understanding, should be stretched like the gooey candy at our old-fashioned taffy pull. Make the audience wait for the emotional payoff.

Heal: The payoff has arrived! The characters reunite, sort through their issues, and embrace a new beginning.

MJ'S HURT-TO-HOPE-TO-HEAL EPISODES

Selina served on the jury that convicted Bart of manslaughter. A year later, another man confessed to the killing, securing Bart's release with a full pardon. Bart eventually found work at Selina's company—as her boss.

Jared was behind the wheel when a truck hit him and his stepsister, Alexa. The accident put Alexa in a wheelchair. Though judged blameless by police, his stepmother Debra destroyed Jared by turning his father, Don, against him. Twenty years later, Don was diagnosed with dementia, and Debra had the nerve to seek Jared's help.

Wyatt returned to his hometown after a fifteen-year absence to teach at his old high school. He soon discovered a student who greatly resembled him, the son of his childhood sweetheart.

People are suckers for the mending of a broken heart—guaranteed!

EYE OF THE BEHOLDER
CHARACTER BUILDING EXERCISE

REVEAL DIVERSE POINTS OF VIEW
THROUGH ACTION AND DIALOGUE

ONCE YOU HAVE **A CAST OF CHARACTERS** IN MIND, we've established that developing them into believable, unique personalities through careful choice of names, mannerisms, temperaments, and physical traits is necessary.

The audience must be able to tell them apart.

Here is a fun exercise that features a diverse **Cast of Characters** and utilizes many of our lessons. I've turned them loose in an active situation to help you better understand motivation and measure them for diversity. Note how each character interprets the circumstances in keeping with their unique outlook, background, and age and then behaves accordingly.

Reminder: Showing their nature through dialogue and action instead of **Telling** leaves the sharpest impression and provides the most entertainment value. The more vitality you breathe into characters, the more human and memorable they become to the audience.

Note what each eyewitness observes in the scenario below through a single line of dialogue. Do you believe each one stands apart?

A brazen robber held up the Midtown Bank at gunpoint and got away with the loot. Eyewitnesses gave police the following accounts.

- "He had a serious rash on his neck." Nancy (Nurse)
- "He had giant black boots like Paul Bunyan." Eva (Kindergartener)
- "He wore a tacky green polyester tracksuit." Jose (Fashion Designer)
- "He was young to be wearing a hearing aid." Shirley (Senior Citizen)
- "He'd bitten his fingernails to the quick!" Kayla (Manicurist)
- "He was wearing a cheap gold Timex with a cracked crystal. Dave (Jeweler)
- "He had dog hairs on his jacket." Barbara (Kennel Owner)
- "He tinted his hair red; the roots revealed a dull brown." Jerry (Barber)
- "He looked over the tops of phony thick eyeglasses." Brent (Optician)
- "Blue eyes, thick lips, scar on the left cheek, 5 foot 3." Wes (Bank teller)

WALK A MILE IN MY SHOES

Let's return to that robbery at the Midtown Bank and draw the eye-witnesses into the fray. They will behave under intense pressure and reveal a glimpse of their **True Identities**. Whether proactive or reactive, their choices help define character, allowing the reader to visualize them more clearly.

In fairness to the cast, I've written the scene from an **Omniscient** POV to give them an equal opportunity to shine. Keep in mind that it is morally acceptable for patrons to comply with the robber's de-mands. He is threatening their lives! Any attempt to resist could put everyone in amplified jeopardy. On the other hand, we are operat-ing in the **Special World** versus the **Real World**, so we can reason-ably expect some feats of derring-do under pressure.

"Paul Bunyan's got a gun!" Young Eva squealed.

With a gasp, Kennel Owner Barbara dived out of sight behind a cleaner's cart.

The burly crook angrily whirled around at the teller's cage, wav-ing a revolver. "We coulda done this the quiet way. Now freeze eve-rybody! Hands-up!"

Most patrons froze, shooting their hands in the air. Fashionista Jose, however, chose to reach for Eva and whisk her behind his slen-der frame.

Jose's sudden movement caught Robber's attention. "Hey, pretty boy, I said, *hands up*." Robber then pulled a large sack out of his jacket and half-turned to toss it at Teller Wes. "Quick! Fill this up with big bills. Now, the rest of you start moving over to the far wall. That includes you over by the tree, fancy suit."

With a meek nod, Jeweler Dave edged away from the big potted palm where he'd just surreptitiously deposited his wallet, Rolex, and rings.

Robber divided his attention between Teller Wes and the shuffling group. Senior Citizen Shirley wobbled slightly against her cane. Manicurist Kayla lowered her hands to gently steady the old lady.

"Halt!" Robber barked, causing startled cries and a minor human pileup. "Okay, banker, come round with the sack. Collect everybody's wallets and purses and toss 'em in."

Wes hurried across the polished floor with the cash-heavy sack, his glasses sliding down his sweat-slicked nose. "Please cooperate," he softly begged the sea of angry, betrayed faces. "It's bank policy."

"Bank policy my ass, you ninny," growled Barber Jerry as he reluctantly tossed his wallet into the bag. "Don't you have a single firearm stashed behind the counter? Even I got a Magnum tucked under the sink at my shop."

With a moan, the wobbly Shirley now fully collapsed against Kayla. Robber stepped closer, only to have Shirley swiftly rally and raise her cane to whack the gun from his hand! Robber stumbled. A bullet discharged as the gun bounced to the floor, barely missing an incensed Dave.

"Crazy stupid prune!" Dave screamed at a hard-eyed Shirley before returning to the potted plant housing his valuables.

Meanwhile, yowling Robber lunged for his weapon. Shirley gladly gave him a second whack, this time to his shoulder. Jerry and Optician Brent attempted to subdue him, but he was unstoppable. He grabbed Nurse Nancy as a shield, shoving her aside only when he cleared the entrance. Nancy stumbled back inside the bank lobby, looking grim.

"It appears a win-win," Wes assessed as he hit the silent alarm. "We all appear unscathed, and he left the cash and his weapon behind."

"He left more behind than you think," Nancy huffed. "I just got a better look at his rash, folks. That man has a case of highly contagious measles."

Assignment

Complete the Bank Robbery Worksheet on the next page. Track some of the cast members in the hours after the robbery.

Now, go for the gusto! Drop *your* characters into a similar pressure-sensitive trap and turn them loose. You needn't use an entire cast. Start with three or four characters if that makes the job easier. Inspire each character to interpret the circumstances in keeping with their unique outlook, background, and age and then behave accordingly.

A bank robbery, a locked room, a deserted island, a storm shelter, or a stalled elevator all hold the potential for identity-revealing chaos. Have fun making their personalities "pop" by revealing quirks, fears, and impulsive behavior.

BANK ROBBERY WORKSHEET

A DEEPER DIVE INTO CHARACTER

CHOOSE YOUR FAVORITE CHARACTERS. Track them after the robbery. How do they describe the dramatic occurrence to others? I predict many will rise up as unsung heroes. Remember, impish Eva belongs to someone. Give her a home.

- **NANCY (NURSE)**

- **EVA (KINDERGARTENER)**

- **JOSE (FASHION DESIGNER)**

- **SHIRLEY (SENIOR CITIZEN)**

- **KAYLA (MANICURIST)**

- **DAVE (JEWELER)**

- **BARBARA (KENNEL OWNER)**

- **JERRY (BARBER)**

- **SETH (OPTICIAN)**

- **WES (BANK TELLER)**

TACKLING THE FIRST DRAFT

THE MUSE IS FEARLESS—SET IT FREE!

PREPARE TO DIVE INTO A WRITER'S TRANCE, the process of creating without overthinking or watching the clock.

So, you are ready to unleash the wild mind. Find a quiet space where, hopefully, you won't be interrupted.

Work with the most comfortable tools, a computer or pen and paper. I alternate between them.

Many writers, myself included, call the first draft of their plot a skeleton, a bare-bones version of what happens. Allow your playful muse free reign with little regard to grammar, punctuation, POV, showing, telling, or tense. Those rules will only slow you down.

Everyone's drafting style is unique. Some first drafts are primarily dialogue, some regale from an *Omniscient* perspective, some report in the *First Person,* and some are a method mashup. A first attempt might morph into hundreds of pages or come in on the short side.

No pressure. Find your process. You're writing like nobody's watching, remember?

Hopefully, your first attempt supplies a rough Beginning, Middle, and End. Can't immediately detect the format? No problem. Keep working.

1. Start a second draft, maybe a third, polishing what you have written. (I label and save each draft in a separate file.)

2. If the **Three-Act** structure continues to elude you, pause the draft cycle. Experiment with scene organization. Assign each scene an index card. Using one of the **Three-Act** diagrams in this manual as a guide, position each scene under a **Beginning, Middle,** or **End** heading. Is the balance off? Does any heading have too many cards? Too few cards? If you are an avid reader/showgoer, the artist in you unconsciously tunes in to format all the time. You can probably recognize what is wrong with the bigger picture by shifting the cards around like puzzle pieces, looking for holes in your plot. Expect to add cards and subtract cards during the process. But keep all the cards as you might choose to restore discarded scenes in a later draft.

TRANCE READY

Determine how much prep you believe is necessary to begin.

Options:

Dive into **Storyland** without a life preserver or a compass! Begin the draft without any planning. Perhaps the project is so spontaneous you call your characters A, B, C, D.

Choose a **Concept** and describe your **Hero** and his **Goal.**

Summarize your story in two lines, paragraphs, or pages as if you are pitching it to an editor.

Go large in advance with a detailed **Storyboard.** Assemble a **Cast of Characters.** Map out your plot and assign each scene an index card. Shuffle the cards into a logical timeline and post them on a board (even a square of cardboard works) to guide you.

Warning: You may get a lot of it wrong before you get it right. There might be numerous drafts ahead of you. It is a regular occurrence. But getting that first draft down is an admirable achievement. The story now lives in your heart. It is something you will expand and improve upon. Guaranteed!

HELP! I'M STUCK!

OVERCOMING WRITER'S BLOCK

"Yikes! The page is blank! My whole mind is blank!"

I HAVE BEEN ON MANY INTENSE DEADLINES OVER THE YEARS. And I have endured writer's block on numerous occasions. Most prolific authors will confess to having suffered through an incident or two.

Most importantly, do not shame yourself. At the very worst, tomorrow is another day.

I have separated the dreaded "BLOCKAGE" into two categories.

THE BIG FREEZE
YOUR CREATIVE SPARK DOESN'T IGNITE ON SCHEDULE

It happens. You grab a beverage; you fire up the computer. You feel obligated to write, yet you don't feel the magic. This predicament can transpire for many reasons, such as lack of sleep, stress, or illness. Perhaps no reasonable explanation whatsoever comes to mind. Bottom Line: You have no desire to write. When you try to force it, the results are clumsy or nonexistent.

As a young, freshly published newbie, I often reacted to this catastrophe with guilt, shame, and deep concern. I should be *working* today! My editor is *waiting* for my story. But if it ain't happenin', it ain't happenin'. Your frisky muse is like a mischievous, unpredictable child playing hide-and-seek. The use of force is hardly the best approach to recapturing it. It is better to *coax* your muse back to work.

Over time, I learned a few handy tricks to get back in the groove.

FORGET ABOUT IT!

Forget all about that darn book for a while. Instead, do some of the things nonwriters voluntarily and guiltlessly do all the time.

Go outdoors! Get some fresh air and sunshine. Walk. Garden. Rake. Mow.

- Do a household chore. Vacuum. Fold laundry. Dust something.
- Read a book.
- Watch a movie.
- Nap.
- Visit a coffee shop or library.
- Build a Lego masterpiece.
- Assemble a puzzle.
- Run over to Target to peruse the book department and buy some candy!

If given the space to wander, the subconscious mind works in mysterious and magical ways. But this "unplugged" method takes patience and maybe you're fresh out.

OPTIMAL REMEDY
POLISH THE PAGES YOU HAVE ALREADY WRITTEN

Sometimes, an author can't leave their stalled project behind to relax. They feel most comfortable forging on without a break. If you are in this state of mind, polish your most recent pages. It may be enough to jumpstart the creative flow. Before you know it, you could be forging ahead with renewed enthusiasm. If not, reconsider visiting Target's books!

THE SMALL FREEZE
YOU STALL OUT AT A SPECIFIC POINT IN YOUR PLOT

You come to a sudden halt along the journey. You feel like you've written yourself into a corner and can't see the next twist in the road. You're energized and *want* to write but can't figure out *what* to write.

This problem can happen at any point along the way. Abruptly, you aren't sure how to proceed. And this indecision may not last for just one day. You may remain stuck longer than that. And understandably, anxiety sets in over time.

"How can I NOT know what happens next in my own story? This whole book must be junk! I'm a no-talent bum who soon will be outed for being a fraud."

Self-recrimination threatens to swallow you up, making the situation so much worse.

You can attempt any of the abovementioned offsite activities to nudge your creativity back into gear. Or you can test-drive these options.

WHAT IF? EXERCISE

Doodle on paper for a bit; jot down character names. Begin to play the game of *What If?* with your cast. *What if* this happened to her? *What if* that happened to him? Write down your thoughts, no matter how silly. This exercise can also lead to a fresh avenue and hopefully unlock your block.

PHONE A FRIEND

Bounce the plot dilemma off a trusted buddy to gain a different perspective. Some authors consult other authors. Others turn to intuitive civilians.

SKIP OVER THE CHALLENGING SCENE

Skip ahead to the next scene if you can visualize it. You can eventually circle back to fill in the blank space. Sometimes, leaping forward gives you better insight into what should have happened in the past.

OPTIMAL REMEDY
DIVE DEEPER INTO CHARACTER

The following technique works best in later, more detailed drafts when you know your characters well.

I suggest tackling this exercise with a pen and paper, but the choice is yours. Briefly abandoning the keyboard as you struggle can take some pressure off you. The sweep of the pen can be more calming than the tap of keys. Also, studies suggest that cursive writing provides a better connection to the brain's creative center, which could lead to better results. No matter how you choose to continue, the first order of business is to close your story file. This is a separate assignment —with no revisions, no additions, no deletions. You won't directly tamper with your story as you explore scene options.

This task is labor-intensive and detailed. In other words—hard work! But the good news is, it is low-stress and can be fun.

Remember: You have left your manuscript behind.

1. List all the characters you could put in the upcoming scene.
2. Briefly review what each of them has been up to recently in the storyline.
3. Examine how each character perceives the *Hero.* Label their current emotional connection. Anger? Joy? Frustration?

Affection? Is anyone poised to interact with the **Hero** in a way that could propel the plot forward?

Nothing yet? Are you still feeling stuck?

Leave the Hero in the wings and draw other Cast Members centerstage.

Mix it up by matching unlikely characters together in conversation. Any chance they could spark a new event? If so, you will have to somehow play out the scene through the viewpoint of one of your chosen narrators. But you probably can find a way to do it!

All is not lost if you allow yourself to stumble a bit as you recalibrate. It's like making a souffle or hanging wallpaper; nobody needs to know what torment you endured to get the job done right.

FIND YOUR TRIBE

WRITING IS A SOLITARY PROFESSION, but you needn't feel alone. While you probably prefer to write in seclusion, connecting with other authors outside work can be very beneficial.

People who work in a communal setting take collective support, in-office comradery, the continual flow of intel, and the goodie table for granted. We need this socialization, too! But we must try harder than the other guys to achieve it. We must reach out to form communities of our peers. But believe me, it is worth it!

WE'RE IN THIS TOGETHER
AND THERE IS SO MUCH TO SHARE

Technical Advice: When you have a computer hardware or software issue, someone in your group will likely have a solution or know someone who can help you. This generosity also applies to the rules of writing. Authors are ordinarily generous with grammar, structure, and plotting knowledge.

Emotional Support: A cheering crew awaits as you celebrate sales and awards and mourn lost opportunities and rejection letters. The submission process is a rollercoaster of emotional highs and lows. My rote answer to editors, producers, and agents who reject my colleagues: *"Your loss, fool!"* We all feel better for saying it out loud.

Creative Guidance: Once your writer relationships feel solid, you may feel comfortable bouncing story ideas off one another. This exchange may or may not lead to plotting sessions where the group helps plot an entire story.

Eventually, you may decide to critique each other's work to gauge reader reaction. This process is a risk and an experiment. Some authors cannot set aside prejudices to evaluate another's effort or respect another's unique voice. This abuse can hurt. However, you won't know who is good at critiquing unless you try it. One way to test the waters is to hold an open forum where authors read a scene or two aloud and invite verbal feedback. The other way is to share a few written pages and invite an edit.

Note that you don't have to accept anyone's criticism. You make the last call on all your creative choices. Also, note that it helps if your critique partners function at your skill level or above. Keep your group small for personal edits; three to six authors work well, but even one trusted advisor can be beneficial.

Caution: Never feel pressured to share your ideas or project details.

Many authors prefer to join in the community fun and forego exchanging work. There is always the chance, however slim, that someone might steal a concept from you. Sorry to say, it happens. I advise you to befriend writers and use your instincts to measure their integrity before handing over chapters and synopses.

Gossip: There is a good kind of gossip: Industry news. It's great to share leads on which agents are looking for clients and which publishers are looking for submissions. There also are lots of contests out there. It's always wonderful to win an award for your novel or script.

Just Plain Fun: Socializing with your own kind lifts the spirits. Colleagues get why you spend ten minutes searching for the ideal synonym!

SEEK OUT SUPPORT

National writers' organizations found online can be helpful. Just make sure they are reputable and established. *Mystery Writers of America, Sisters in Crime, Science Fiction & Fantasy Writers Association, and Poets & Writers, Inc.* are several to consider. They typically have membership fees, but receiving a newsletter and a communication network from the deal can make it worthwhile. If you can only join one organization, choose one closely connected to your chosen genre, such as mystery/suspense, science fiction, young adult, or romance. Many of these national groups have local chapters—another plus!

Do you prefer a less structured situation? There are local writers casually meeting all over the place, such as libraries, schools, homes, restaurants, and bookstores—and they often charge no dues. It's a matter of asking the right person for a lead. Teachers, guidance counselors, and school office personnel are valuable resources, as are librarians and booksellers. A nice thing about many small informal groups is that they aren't necessarily genre-specific. They often welcome writers from a variety of categories. And befriending writers in various genres will help broaden your scope.

THAT'S ALL SHE WROTE

THANKS FOR STOPPING BY

THIS MANUAL WAS A JOY TO WRITE. As with all writing projects, it was a challenging adventure. I expected to complete it in two months. In the spirit of following my muse, it took me *ten* months!

I worked hard to assemble my thoughts in a user-friendly format. It was a labor of love for my talented family—anyone who dreams of writing a story. I wish you the best of luck!

MJ'S CAFÉ TAKEAWAY

- *Storytelling is an exciting adventure.*

- *Like any great hero, be alert, available, and open to change.*

- *Seek out methods that work for you.*

- *Embrace your unique voice.*

- *"Peek under the hood" of your favorite works to study what makes them tick.*

- *Create memorable characters.*

- *Expect to do rewrites.*

- *Welcome edits: they make you stronger.*

- *Be curious—you never know where inspiration will spark.*

ABOUT THE AUTHOR

MJ SCHULTZ OFTEN WRITES UNDER THE PENNAME LEANDRA LOGAN. She is a bestselling author published in various genres, including romance, mystery, young adult, and illustrated books for children. MJ is a multi-Romantic Times Awards winner and has received numerous nominations within the industry. Her critics praise her for her deeply emotional stories, often lightened with humor, and the red herrings she thoroughly enjoys planting to keep her readers guessing.

You can reach her at: mjswriterscafe@gmail.com

www.ingramcontent.com/pod-product-compliance
Lightning Source LLC
Chambersburg PA
CBHW062137020426
42335CB00013B/1244